Nine Lives

Episodes in an Australian
Foreign Service Career

Other Connor Court Books
on Australia's International Relations

Jeremy Hearder, *Jim Plim – Ambassador Extraordinary*

John Burgess, *The Solidarity Challenge, 1980-82*

NINE LIVES

EPISODES IN AN AUSTRALIAN FOREIGN SERVICE CAREER

Richard Gate

Connor Court Publishing

Published in 2019 by Connor Court Publishers Pty Ltd.

Copyright © Richard Gate

Not to be reproduced without the permission of the Copyright holders.

Connor Court Publishing Pty Ltd.
PO Box 7257
Redland Bay QLD 4165
sales@connorcourt.com
www.connorcourt.com

ISBN: 9281925826463

Cover Design by Maria Giordano

Printed in Australia.

Contents

Foreword
The Honourable Justice T. M. Thawley
Federal Court of Australia — vii

Prelude — xi

1 Foreign Service, 1940-70 — 1

2. KOREA, 1958-60
   The Fall of President Syngman Rhee — 7

3. ISRAEL, 1963-65
   Changing Attitudes — 37

4. KENYA, 1965-68
   Post-Colonial Afterglow — 55

5. NAURU, 1970-72
   A Pacific Paradise? — 73

6. ITALY, 1974-77
   Will Italy go Communist? — 83

7. BURMA, 1980-82
   Before Aung San Suu Kyi — 95

8. JORDAN, 1982-85
   At the Court of a King — 119

9. NEW ZEALAND, 1986-88
   A Degree of Estrangement   135

10. BANGLADESH, 1989-93
    An Unexpected Revolution   143

11. Afterlife   183

    Acknowledgements   185

FOREWORD

The Honourable Justice T. M. Thawley
Federal Court of Australia

Richard began his overseas career in the Foreign Service on 2 June 1958 when he arrived in Seoul. Richard was Australia's Alternative Representative to the United Nations Commission for the Unification and Rehabilitation of Korea ("UNCURK", although referred to by the North Koreans as the "fig leaf of democracy"). Richard held the rank of Third Secretary. His insightful dispatches to Canberra began.

It was five years after the end of the Korean war. Syngman Rhee, who had first been elected President of the Republic of Korea in 1948, won his fourth term in office in 1960. He sought also to inflict his friend, "the syphilitic Lee Ki-poong", on the electorate as Vice-President. The election was rigged. President Rhee "won" 90% of the vote and Lee Ki-poong also won by a large margin. These events triggered the April Revolution in which Syngman Rhee was driven from his Presidential mansion into exile. Marshall Green, Counsellor in the American Embassy in Seoul, observed that "you can't sail the ship of State with a Lee Ki-poong".

Richard's last posting was as High Commissioner to Bangladesh from 1989 to 1993. He was supposed to have been Ambassador to Syria, but they would not have him on account of his having been posted to Israel, with whom Syria was at war. In Bangladesh, he witnessed the eight day revolution which brought down the military Government of Lieutenant General Ershad.

In the thirty years between these two revolutions, Richard had seven postings, three as head of mission. Apart from South Korea and Bangladesh, he was posted to Israel (1963-1965), Kenya (1965-1968), Nauru (1970-1972), Italy (1974-1977), Burma

(1980-1982), the Hashemite Kingdom of Jordan (as he likes to refer to it) (1982-1985) and New Zealand (1986). It was in New Zealand that he did his Master's degree on his time in the Middle East. Asked how he did it, he said gruffly: "between nine and twelve on Sunday mornings".

Richard was posted to Italy, as Counsellor, in 1974. He succeeded the formidable Mary McPherson. The flamboyant John Ryan was Ambassador. Luckily for me, Richard lived in a grand old apartment in the English College upstairs from us, my father having been posted to Rome in 1973.

Rome suited Richard with his deep love of art and music. He knew where every Caravaggio was located. His capacity to visit them, repeatedly, exceeds that of any other human being. He would go to the concerts at Santa Cecilia. He was once observed to lean across to prevent, with a deep growl, the continued rustling by an Italian woman of her cough lollies. He developed a love of Italian food, but no knowledge of how to cook it.

Postings were not always comfortable, even in Rome. It was the time of the "Brigate Rosse"; there were riots in the streets. Aldo Moro, leader of the Christian Democrats, was Prime Minister. Italy was teetering on the edge of communism; the Christian Democrats and Communists were roughly equal in the polls.

Gough Whitlam, then Prime Minister of Australia, John Ryan and Aldo Moro met and were photographed during Whitlam's visit to Rome. His planned tour of the sights of Sicily was abruptly cancelled because of Cyclone Tracy in Darwin. Richard points out that fate is sometimes cruel. Whitlam lasted as Prime Minister until 11 November 1975. The Red Brigades kidnapped Aldo Moro, who was found assassinated in the boot of a car 59 days later. John Ryan's career ended prematurely after the notorious raid on the Sheraton Hotel in Melbourne. Ryan, then head of ASIS, authorised the raid as a training exercise. Richard, a very sober and strategic thinker, would have done no such thing.

FOREWORD

One of Richard's greatest charms is that he can laugh at himself. Another is that he is a wonderful mimic. Under his gentle exterior, however, is a serious and acute observer, ever on the watch for the vagaries of human or government behaviour. Someone once said he had only ever met three truly cultured people in Foreign Affairs, one of whom was Sir James Plimsoll, the other Richard Gate; and I have forgotten the third. There are of course many more, but it is remarkable how Richard has kept up his interests in art and music, travelling the world still several times a year at the age of eighty-five, producing his own music program and writing articles for learned magazines. His reading is prolific and focussed and his judgment on foreign issues is always sharp. He is immensely curious. He is not satisfied with what he knows, nor are his opinions written in stone. He has always had enthusiasm for new adventures. He saw each country he was posted to as a wonderful opportunity.

Richard's accounts of his postings are stamped with his hallmark: a deeply perceptive and lively account of the social, economic and political significance of his experiences.

His superb understanding of politics, music and art stands in complete contrast to his total inability to understand a film plot.

But Richard has a greater quality than all of those just mentioned. He is both loving and kind.

It is a great honour to be able to commend *Nine Lives* to readers.

Prelude

Sir Arthur Tange, the longest serving Secretary of the Department of External Affairs (later the Department of Foreign Affairs and even later the Department of Foreign Affairs and Trade) once said that "the job of this Department is the conduct of Australia's overseas public business". For officers serving in Australia's foreign missions, this includes a wide variety of duties – negotiations with the host government on matters of mutual interest, promotion of trade, defence and security issues, consular matters involving Australians visiting the host country, issuing visas to Australia, promotion of cultural ties, public information activities. There is also the task of reporting on the economic, political and social developments in the countries concerned. To do this latter task properly, the mission must have access to key people in the country who can brief officers on such developments. In addition, there is the task of administering the mission efficiently and with integrity.

In most smaller posts, these tasks are undertaken by officers of the Department of Foreign Affairs and Trade, those in what used to be called the diplomatic stream and the consular and administrative stream. In bigger posts, where circumstances warrant it, the mission will also include officers from the departments and agencies concerned with immigration, health and officers from the Defence Force.

Officers are provided with furnished accommodation. Local allowances are also paid in expensive cities to cover the higher cost of living. There are also representation allowances to enable officers to entertain local personalities who can provide information about the countries concerned. Arrangements are also made to meet, at least partially, the costs of school fees. In very difficult posts, the costs of holidays to appropriate, more comfortable, leave centres are also met. Home leave is granted at least once during a posting. In posts with no or difficult transport systems, officers are driven to work. Provision is also made for officers to have domestic assistance; this is particularly necessary for officers who have representational duties at home. Such assistance is, however, a mixed blessing. One Secretary of the Department once commanded that "a way must be found – and it must be found – to stop people being driven mad by servants". It never was found.

Officers are not under any obligation to pay local taxes, nor can they be prosecuted for infringing local laws. This does not mean, however, that they can flout these laws deliberately. Anyone who did so frequently would eventually be returned to Canberra and subject to some disciplinary action. Probably the most useful result of the freedom from local taxation is the ability to buy cars free of sales tax. Some countries build GST-type taxes into the prices of all goods and services and claim they must be paid by members of foreign missions; this can lead to difficulties with host governments;

A normal posting of three or four years enables officers to become closely acquainted with political, economic and social conditions in the country concerned. Sometimes this can lead officers to develop views of the country that are at odds with the current view, or policy, held in Canberra. It can also lead them to hold views that are at odds with the views of other officers in the same mission. Such situations must be delicately dealt with if tensions are not to arise within the embassy or with Canberra.

It is also necessary always to view developments in the host country as a whole. It is useless to pursue some trade or cultural policy if it is at variance with the overall policy of the host government or development within the host country.

Officers need to be informed of events and activity in Australia. I remember one instance when a Head of Mission, who had not been reading the Australian press, was embarrassed when a visiting minister from Australia was caught up in a parliamentary crisis of which the Head of Mission was ignorant.

An important task is the handling of visitors including the Prime Minister, other ministers, heads of department and other agencies, junior officers from departments, journalists, businessmen, parliamentarians and individual travellers. Appointments must be made and a member of the mission delegated to accompany the visitor on his or her calls. These programs usually work well enough, but there can be difficulties, particularly in the case of very high level visitors such as the Prime Minister or the Foreign Minister, if the Head of Mission does not know the visitor and is therefore unaware of the visitor's idiosyncrasies. On one occasion, a minister I escorted to call on the President of the host country opened the conversation by urging the President to give the press greater latitude. There was no reason to say this as the press was comparatively free. One Foreign Minister refused to be entertained at the official residence; another demanded to come and to be served local food. Businessmen often want to be accompanied by their local representative when they call on the Head of Mission; this means that the latter cannot speak as freely as he might wish. Some businessmen have been known to complain that the mission was not giving sufficient courtesy to their local representative.

Colleagues in other missions are useful in assessing important developments in the host country. Usually the British and American embassies are the most useful because they are interested in the same things which interest Australian officers. The Americans are usually the best informed on current developments. The British, who were previously the rulers in four of the countries in which I served, take a more historical and long term view. Other embassies can be useful depending on the particular interests of the Ambassador. Sometimes they have other interests which are not the same as ours. One Ambassador from a European country was mainly concerned with imports of red earth which were of little interest to Australia.

Writing memoirs about diplomatic life is not straightforward. There is no point in simply repeating a narrative of facts that can be found in a history book. On the other hand, too personal an account will give the impression that the writer spent time frivolously without regard to serious events taking place. In this book I have tried to keep my eye on the general picture, but also to write about what interested me and give local colour to life in a diplomatic post.

The book is designed to give some idea of what happens in an Australian mission overseas. It is not a history of the particular countries concerned, nor is it a full account of Australian relations with those countries. It is an account of the happenings that I experienced and what my reactions were to them.

1
FOREIGN SERVICE, 1940-70

"Korea is the best kept secret in Canberra" remarked the Australian major attached to the United Nations Command in Korea in 1959, the second year of my posting there. Indeed, in those days, Seoul and Jakarta were considered the most uncomfortable posts in Australia's infant but developing foreign service. The Korean War had finished only five years previously, living conditions were thought to be primitive, the climate, with freezing winters and stifling summers, difficult and we did not yet have an embassy there. I was a member of the Australian Delegation to the United Nations Commission for the Unification and Rehabilitation of Korea (UNCURK).

It soon became obvious that I could not have had a better posting to begin my career. The intelligence and charm of the Korean people, the dramatic political developments that took place when I was there, the interest in working in a United Nations field mission and the beauties of Korean arts were as good as I could have experienced anywhere.

It was not my first time overseas. Born in Brisbane, I had grown up in Canberra but, in 1945, when I was twelve, my father, who, working for the old Department of Trade and Customs, had been posted to New York where we remained until 1950. I had most of my secondary education there and, after finishing at Canberra High School, I started a six-year course at Melbourne University in Arts and Law. I studied Australian history, British history, Ancient history, American history and Theory and Method of History. Curiously, it was Australian history with which I had the most difficulty. My five years in America had not prepared me for it; there seemed to be no good text books and, on the whole,

I found the subject rather dull. My most memorable teachers were Professors R. M. Crawford, Norman Harper, Kathleen Fitzpatrick in history and Professor Zelman Cowen, Dr Norval Morris and H. A. J. Ford in law.

After four years, when I had finished the Arts course and two years of the Law course, I joined the then Department of External Affairs (as Foreign Affairs was then known) in 1956 and never finished Law. The only "international" activity I indulged in at the university was organising each year, for three years, fairs on the university grounds to raise funds to build International House which still stands on Sydney Road. We raised about four thousand pounds each year, a substantial amount in those days. In 1954 I had made a brief journey during the summer holidays to New Caledonia, with two university friends including the future Senator John Button. The rest of the time during the summer I earned money by cleaning windows and other pursuits.

Those years in New York were when the post-war world was created, the Cold War began, the United Nations was founded, Churchill made his famous Iron Curtain speech at Fulton, Missouri, the Berlin Airlift took place, Czechoslovakia fell to communism, Yugoslavia broke with the Comintern, the Chinese communists triumphed and established the People's Republic of China and the war against the French in Indo-China began. All these matters attracted much attention in the United States and were reported and commented on fully in the media. One consequence for myself was that I never was attracted to any form of communism.

By the time I returned to Australia, I had some idea of what had happened in Asia since the Second World War and realised developments there could be of serious concern to Australia. Not long afterwards the Korean War broke out.

When I joined the Department of Foreign Affairs in 1956, there was no doubt that Asia was the main focus of Australian diplomacy. The situation in the countries between Australia and Communist China (which was hostile to Western countries including Australia) was not re-assuring. Their economies were primitive and their societies unstable. Poverty was widespread. In Indo-China, the French were fighting a nationalist movement supported by communism. There was a revolutionary movement, also communist, in the Philippines. Power in Indonesia was divided between the army, on the one hand, and the Communist Party on the other; President Sukarno was an unpredictable umpire. A catastrophe was expected there and it came in 1965, although with better eventual results for Australia than expected. There was a strong anti-Western communist insurgent movement in Malaya (later Malaysia). Burma, although possessing a democratic government, was ravaged by innumerable insurgent movements; its future was most uncertain.

Australian leaders knew, and the Australian public accepted, that we could not turn our eyes away from Asia, ignore developments there and continue to rely on links with Europe and America. Countries which adopted policies that neglected their own immediate area, such as Israel and South Africa, eventually had to abandon them.

Our priority during the 1950s was to win acceptance of Australia in the region so that we could become a serious partner in efforts to improve conditions in South-East Asia. The then Minister for External Affairs, R. G. Casey, travelled extensively throughout the area and established good relations with Asian leaders. We sent good ambassadors and high commissioners into the area who did the same. These included W. R. Crocker and Peter Heydon in India, J. D. L. Hood and later Crocker in Indonesia, Major-General Walter Cawthorn in Pakistan, T. K. Critchley in Malaya, K. C. O. Shann in the Philippines and later Indonesia, and F. J. Blakeney in Vietnam. By 1960 we were, on the whole, well regarded in Asia. I was to serve later under both Hood and Crocker both of whom had had extensive international experience, Hood as a leader writer for the London *Times* and Crocker in the British colonial service and army and at the United Nations. Cawthorn had been in the army and both Heydon and Shann had had long diplomatic experience. Heydon later became Secretary of the Department of Immigration and Shann Chairman of the Public Service Board and subsequently a member of the Board of Mount Isa Mining.

The main purpose of our policy was to help to foster conditions in Asia which would lead to economic progress and social stability. There is no doubt that this effort succeeded, although it is difficult to assess how much this was due to our efforts. Economic development of Indonesia, Malaysia, Singapore, Thailand, Korea, Taiwan, even Vietnam and India exceeded all our expectations. We never dreamt that the leader of one of these countries, Lee Kuan Yew, would one day refer to us as the "poor white trash of Asia".

All newly-recruited foreign service officers expected their first posting to be in Asia (although this did not always eventuate). Asia was where the action was and was the best place in which to learn our craft. I participated in the United Nations Commission in Korea; one of my colleagues helped to draft the Malayan Constitution; another, slightly later, played a role that is still remembered locally in the establishment of Bangladesh.

Our training for such assignments was haphazard. The Department had genuine difficulty (a difficulty that has persisted) in deciding what form of training was the best. We undertook various ad hoc courses at the Canberra University College and special courses in such matters as international law were arranged for us internally. The relevance of these courses sometimes seemed doubtful. Desk work in the Department did not always prepare us for Asia. Some officers worked, for example, in the Consular and Protocol Branch or the Middle East Branch and were then sent to Asia without any specific training for that area. We spent hours learning such tedious tasks as how to envelope secret documents.

I worked first in the Colombo Plan Branch for about six months, then in the Branch dealing with the South-East Asian Treaty Organization (SEATO) for about a year. SEATO had been established by the United States, France, Australia, the United Kingdom, Thailand, Pakistan and the Philippines following the French defeat in Vietnam in 1954. It was intended to be a bulwark against communism in South-East Asia. Finally, before I went on my first posting to Korea, I worked in the South-East Asia Branch.

In the Colombo Plan Branch, I dealt with the training of Asian students in Australia, particularly with their welfare and accommodation, the provision of Australian experts to Colombo Plan countries and the supply of capital equipment. Dealing with students, we had to make sure they were treated properly in Australia, which was not used to young Asian visitors, and that Australians had some understanding of their personal expectations.

At the same time, we had to introduce the students to the Australian way of life. This was not always easy. They had difficulty understanding, for example, why, although it was impossible to buy a newspaper or anything else on Sunday (a holdover from Sabbatarianism), it was acceptable for women to smoke in public (in their eyes, a display of wantonness).

In the SEATO Branch, I was concerned with supply of Australian economic assistance to the Asian members of SEATO – Pakistan, the Philippines and Thailand, originally called "twilight aid" because it fell into a category somewhere between economic assistance and defence assistance. When I moved to the South-East Asia Branch, I was mainly concerned with Laos which even at that stage seemed to be slipping inevitably into communist rule. Cambodia looked fairly stable under Sihanouk and even Vietnam was not overtly the mess it became in later years. Nevertheless, there was a sense of unease about Indo-China and it was difficult to believe that the leaders who looked to the West in those countries had much chance of survival. I also dealt with Burma and it seemed to be accepted wisdom that Burma, too, would eventually become a puppet state of China. The outlook for South-East Asia in 1958 was not encouraging.

Very little of the training that I had had in the Department was directly relevant to my first posting in Korea, for which I had only about two or three months' notice. I knew the general directions of Australian foreign policy; I knew how to send a telegram and compose a memorandum; I knew how to operate the filing system and manage accounts. Most important, I knew how to type; there was no permanent secretarial clerical assistance in Seoul.

2

KOREA, 1958-60

The Fall of President Syngman Rhee

My first encounter with Asia was on 2 June 1958, the day I arrived in Seoul as Alternate Representative of Australia to the United Nations Commission for the Unification and Rehabilitation of Korea (UNCURK), with the rank of Third Secretary. (A Third Secretary was, among diplomatic staff, the humblest rank. After rising to Second, then First Secretary, the next rank on the ladder was Counsellor. Heads of Mission, either Ambassadors or High Commissioners, were drawn from among Counsellors, in appropriate cases, on promotion.)

It took some time to reach Korea. Planes were slow in those days and the Department was generous in letting officers stop over en route. My first stop was Saigon, then untroubled by the forthcoming war. Next, I was in Hong Kong to do some shopping and to order some suits and table ware. I then spent several days in Tokyo where I met the then Ambassador, Sir Alan Watt, formerly Secretary of the Department (1950-54) and a Rhodes Scholar, and other officers on whom we often depended for logistical help. Sir Alan's previous postings included ambassadorship in Moscow and a position as roving envoy in South-East Asia with residence in Singapore. Later he became Ambassador to the Federal Republic of Germany.

I was met in Seoul by the Australian Representative on UNCURK, Hugh Dunn, a Queensland Rhodes Scholar and future Ambassador to both the Republic of China and the People's Republic of China, his wife and my predecessor, Robin Ashwin, another Rhodes Scholar. They escorted me to my house in the foreigners' section of Seoul, Itaewon. UNCURK itself was located in an ersatz Rhenish castle, built by a Korean nobleman with a penchant for everything German, on a hill near the President's palace. When I visited Korea in 1990, I found it had been burnt down.

Although some Australian politicians have in recent decades claimed that it was only they who discovered Asia, the fact is that Asia was already important to Australia. We had already fought two wars in Asia (1941-45) and in Korea (1950-53) and before long would be fighting in another (Vietnam). A first posting in Asia was considered highly desirable to enable young officers to become familiar with this area of greatest interest to Australia.

Because we were part of a United Nations Commission, we were paid what was then the princely sum of $US20 a day (tax free) by the United Nations. The Australian Government did not pay staff allowances (we did receive salaries) and took no responsibility for our accommodation, personal or otherwise. The United Nations provided the delegation with a car and, during my time, the Australian Government did eventually provide a Land Rover. After a great deal of argument, the Australian Cabinet, no less, agreed that Hugh Dunn, the first married Representative, should be paid a small living allowance. I paid my representation expenses from the United Nations allowance, and had to find and pay for my own housing. Although these arrangements were anomalous, I could not complain. I managed to live off the United Nations allowance and save my salary the entire time I was in Korea. When I returned to Australia after two-and-a-half years, I had saved two and a half thousand pounds – a very nice sum to have so early in life.

Accommodation proved a problem. I first occupied my predecessor's house in Itaewon. The houses had been built in "Western style" by the Korean Housing Administration, but were hot in summer and cold in winter when heating costs were high. I was constantly bothered by a rat which spent each night trying to chew through the kitchen door into the dining room. In the mornings I was awakened by a loudspeaker from a nearby army camp bawling physical education instructions to the young recruits. After nine months, I moved to an apartment house dating from Japanese times. It was cheaper and nearer the office but I could never manage to have a telephone installed and this made life difficult. After six months, I rented a more stylish house from an Italian businessman in a more up-market, Korean part of town. Again the rent and heating costs were high, but at least I could entertain more easily.

For my final last nine months in Korea, I lived in a small apartment overlooking the beautiful Han River which flows through Seoul. As this period coincided with political upheavals, when we were all very busy, the fact that entertaining was less easy did not matter so much. In this apartment, I was awoken at night by trains which rushed past nearby.

The Australian Government's main interest politically and strategically in those days was South-East Asia, particularly Malaya, Singapore, the Philippines, Indo-China and Indonesia. The Indian sub-continent attracted slightly less interest. Japan, economically important, was then a political pygmy. Korea, although the scene of a war in which we had fought, was not of primary importance to us. Strategically, it was the responsibility of the United States and offered little to us economically; trade barely existed. Politically, President Syngman Rhee's Government was considered authoritarian and unpredictable and was not on good terms with other Asian governments whose friendship we were seeking. Australia contributed to the United Nations' aid programs, but did not have any direct aid programs of its own for Korea. Most Australian aid at that time was directed to Colombo Plan countries; Korea had never been a member of the Colombo Plan.

Partly for these reasons, Australia did not even have an embassy or a legation in Korea. An AIF major accredited to the United Nations Command was the only visible reminder of our participation in the Korean War. Consular matters were undertaken and visas to Australia were issued by the British Embassy. Although we were not accredited to the Korean Government, it did accept us as the voice of the Australian Government but only in an informal sense. We could not make formal representations to the Foreign Ministry. Administrative problems were the responsibility of the UNCURK Secretariat. The Delegation itself had no administrative assistance and we had no clerical support until after I arrived when we recruited a local Australian resident as a typist. Several months later, the Australian Government did at last despatch a typist from the Department to assist us. She was Joyce Bull, already famous for her assistance as a QANTAS hostess to Mrs Petrov when the latter was saved from forced repatriation to Moscow in 1954 after the espionage crisis of that year. Nevertheless, despite all these anomalies, the position I held was a responsible one and it was considered something of a compliment be sent there, for reasons explained below.

A session of the United Nations Commission for the Unification and Rehabilitation of Korea

KOREA, 1958-60

Korea seemed in those days to be a country without a future. The population was 22 million. Economically, it was kept going by annual infusions of American aid to the value of about $275-$300 million (a much more significant amount in those days than it would be now). The country grew enough rice to feed itself, but little was left over for export; there were in any case no export markets. Manufacturing had only just begun and nothing of export quality was produced. It seemed as if Korea's only exports would be such things as nuts, seaweed, fruit and fish. These did not bring in much return. One statistic that has always stuck in my mind is that, in 1959, Korea's total exports amounted to no more than $US 19 million.

Seoul itself, except for the damage done in the war, remained much as it had been in the final days of Japanese rule. All infrastructure, public buildings and upper-class residential quarters had been built by the Japanese and gave the city a quaint, old-fashioned look. To his credit, President Syngman Rhee had managed to keep the framework of the country going: the trains ran on time and were efficient; telecommunications were reasonable; the press was flourishing and, to a surprising degree, there was freedom of expression; Seoul was served by regular flights from Tokyo and Hong Kong; there was no shortage of food. Roads were rough and unsealed, but all of the country was traversable by car. The standard of living for the Korean people, especially those in rural areas, was very low.

Korea had been divided along the 38th parallel in 1945 when the surrender of Japanese forces was accepted by Soviet forces in the north and by American forces in the south. This division subsequently became frozen after the establishment of the Russian-backed Democratic People's Republic of Korea in the north and the Western-backed Republic of Korea in the south.

In June 1950 North Korean forces attacked the south, leading to the intervention by sixteen nations, led by the United States, authorised by Resolution 83 of the United Nations Security Council of 27 June 1950.

UNCURK had been later established by the General Assembly of the United Nations (Resolution 376(V) of 7 October 1950) to promote the United Nations' objectives of bringing about, by peaceful means, the establishment of a unified, independent and democratic Korea under a representative form of government. At that time, because of the advance by the United Nations forces into North Korea, the end of the war and the subsequent unification of the country seemed to be in sight. China's entry into the war late in 1950 ended that prospect. UNCURK's mandate to unify the country evaporated, for the time being anyway.

By the time I arrived in Seoul, UNCURK's role was limited essentially to two tasks. One task each year was to write a report to the General Assembly which included a chapter on the Development of Representative Government in Korea. The other was to observe elections of national scope (that is, elections that took place in South Korea, as North Korea did not allow us to visit that country).

Democracy had developed only with difficulty in Korea. When I arrived in Korea, the Korean Constitution provided for an executive presidential system. President Syngman Rhee, whose patriotism and ability were beyond question, had become the nation's first President in 1948 and had been president ever since.

President Rhee was born in 1875. He converted to Methodism at an early age. He was imprisoned by the then Korean Government in 1898 for anti-government activities and left Korea in 1904 for the United States where he studied at George Washington University and Harvard. He then obtained a doctorate from Princeton in 1910, the year that Japan annexed Korea. The subject of his dissertation was "Neutrality as influenced by the United States." He was the first Korean to obtain a Ph D from an American university. He remained overseas for many years, marrying an

Austrian, Francesca Donner, in 1934. He was selected by General MacArthur as a potential Korean leader. After a bloody election for a parliament, Rhee was elected President of the Republic of Korea by the parliament in 1948.

Elections had traditionally been marked by violence. President Rhee resorted to extreme ends to maintain his rule; in 1952, when it appeared that the National Assembly might not re-elect him to another term, he declared Martial Law. Rhee won that particular round, but he appeared threatened again in 1956 when, the Constitution having been amended to provide for popular election of the president, he was challenged by the popular Patrick Henry Shinicky. Fortunately for President Rhee, Shinicky died during the election campaign, but his running mate, Dr John M. Chang, was elected Vice-President. President Rhee regarded Dr Chang's election as a personal insult to him and refused to work with the new Vice-President.

UNCURK's task of observing and reporting on elections and other political developments to the General Assembly gave UNCURK some standing and made it an object of attention to both the Government and its opponents. UNCURK's reports were accepted in the United Nations and other circles as giving an accurate account of what was happening politically in Korea. United Nations' decisions about Korea, and the decisions of individual Western governments, which were important to the Korean Government, would be made, to some extent, on the basis of what we wrote.

Because of the nature of UNCURK's mandate, it had always, even in those early days, been concerned with human rights, particularly development of representative government and the role of a free press. These matters were the central concern of our report each year to the General Assembly. In some cases, UNCURK took up the case of individual rights. As the first Australian Representative, James Plimsoll had made very firm representations to President Rhee during the political crisis of 1952 when the latter had victimised some of his political enemies.

One point which gave added tang to our work was that the South Korean Government openly advocated a "march north" policy to unify the country and rather resented the United Nations policy of unification by peaceful means. North Korea seemed to have a similar "march south" policy. The result was an atmosphere of constant tension; one could never be sure that war would not break out at any minute. We understood that the United States, whose Eighth Army was permanently stationed in Korea, kept the Korean army deliberately on low supplies of petrol to prevent a southern invasion of the North.

UNCURK membership originally comprised seven countries – Australia, Chile, the Netherlands, Pakistan, Philippines, Thailand and Turkey. When, however, UNCURK's priority task of unifying the country became unattainable, the Commission reduced itself in 1955 to a committee of four – Australia, the Philippines, Thailand and Turkey. The other three countries retained their membership and were occasionally represented at meetings of the Commission in Seoul by their ambassadors in Tokyo.

In the early days of UNCURK, Australian representation had been at a senior level. Its first Australian member was James Plimsoll, later Secretary of the Department of External Affairs (1965-70). By 1958, however, the Australian Government had concluded that UNCURK no longer required such senior representation. The Representative now had the rank of Second Secretary, and the Alternate that of Third Secretary. Most of the other members of the Commission were more senior in their own services than we were, and this sometimes led to difficulties, particularly as the Australians were, on the whole, the most active members of UNCURK.

Another problem was that some of the other countries, such as Pakistan and Turkey, also had encountered problems along the road to democracy and this complicated their attitude towards, and their willingness to comment on, development of democracy in Korea. Nevertheless, despite our junior status, both the Representative and the Alternate had to be fairly mature and responsible officers who could represent Australia without the guidance of a senior resident ambassador.

Even so, our anomalous position caused some problems. The Minister for External Affairs, Casey, visited Korea in 1959. He accepted the British Ambassador's invitation to stay at the British Embassy. Although this was proper, as it was legitimate for the Australian Minister to stay in the Queen's house in Seoul in the absence of an Australian Embassy, it limited our access to the minister. When the Australian Representative on UNCURK called at the Ambassador's house to pick up Mr and Mrs Casey on the first day of the visit, the Ambassador's wife kept him waiting outside and sharply reprimanded him for calling without an official invitation!

As far as possible, we attempted to show an Australian presence throughout the country. One of my first adventures was in the winter of 1958-59 when I travelled on a Korean naval vessel to the remote island of Ullung-do, in the Sea of Japan, about half way between Korea and Japan.

Ullung-do was a largish island, thickly populated by people who survived largely on fishing. That year the currents in the Sea of Japan had taken an unexpected course and the fishing harvest collapsed, leaving the people with nothing to eat. As usual in such circumstances, the American aid mechanism swung into action and provided a large shipment of food which was taken to the island by the Korean navy. UNCURK was asked to send a representative to watch the proceedings and I volunteered.

The ship sailed from Pusan and took about a day and a night to reach Ullung-do. We arrived in the morning and the plan was that we would unload the food and then leave, after a brief walk through the island, which turned out to be very pretty, and a handover ceremony. Unfortunately, immediately after the latter, rain began to fall and continued, heavily, for eight days.

We were unable to return to the ship which itself could not stay near the island because there was no safe harbour. It returned to Pusan, leaving on the island those of us who had come to watch the handover. They included, in addition to myself, about three others, including two Americans.

We had no money, nor night-attire, change of clothes or toothbrushes. This would have not been too bad had we been on Ullung-do for one or two nights. In the event, we were there for eight nights and became increasingly dirty and unpresentable. We stayed, free of charge, in a small Korean inn which was quite comfortable, although I do not remember what the bathing facilities were like, or even if there were any. The W.C. facilities were primitive, consisting of a somewhat elevated outhouse which seemed undermined and threatened by the heavy rainfall. Every time I used it, I thought the whole thing would collapse, with me on it, into the vast cesspit below.

The manageress of the hotel came in every night formally to see how we were coping. She did not speak English, and we, for our part, had little Korean, but we appreciated her gesture and her hospitality. What was very disheartening was that we were served very good food the whole time we were there. Every night, as I recall, we had roast chicken. We knew that most of the people on the island were starving, but our protestations were to no avail. We were honoured foreign guests and nothing was too good for us.

We found filling in the time difficult. We sat for lengthy periods in the inn reading *LIFE* magazine and a Bible which someone had thoughtfully left. Then, about twice a day, would run down in the rain to the local coffee house. Shaving also presented problems as none of us had razors. We patronised the local barbershop but this proved a most hazardous experience as the barbers were used to the thin elegant beards of Korean gentlemen and not to the thick, coarse growths of Western barbarians. After several frightening attempts by the barber to shave me with a cut-throat, I decided to remain unshaved for the duration of the stay on Ullung-do. Eventually the ship returned and we sailed to Pusan.

Richard Gate (left) and other members of the mission bringing food to the island of Ullung-do

By June 1958, when I arrived, the political scene had to some extent stabilised after the eventful presidential election of 1956. An election had taken place for the National Assembly in May which had gone with little incident. President Rhee's Liberal Party emerged with a safe majority of 126 seats out of 233, but the Democratic Party, the main opposition party, had also done well with 79 seats, an increase of 33. Economic development was progressing as well as it could and the country was gradually recovering from the devastation of the Korean War.

It was increasingly clear, however, that President Rhee was determined to remain in power. He totally ignored the Vice-

President, Dr John M. Chang (from the opposition party), and executed Cho Bong-am, the leader of the Progressive Party, a vaguely left-wing organisation, who had stood against him in 1956 and had won a healthy three million votes. All eyes were focussing on the presidential elections due in 1960 when it was expected that Rhee would run again.

The new National Assembly had a stormy history. Differences between the two main parties centred on the proposal of the Government and the Liberal Party to amend the National Security Law and the Local Autonomy Law. The Government claimed that these amendments were necessary to enable it to deal more effectively with subversive activities in the first case, and to provide a sounder basis for local government in the second. Its opponents claimed that the amendments were intended to restrict the activities of the opposition parties in the 1960 elections.

The opposition refused to accept the proposed amendments and the Government refused to consider any modifications. For some time the opposition attempted to obstruct the workings of the Assembly. Finally, on 24 December 1958, three hundred special guards entered the Assembly Hall, forcibly ejected the opposition members and detained them in the basement. In their absence, the Liberal Party passed more than twenty bills including the 1959 budget and the amended Local Autonomy and National Security laws. The stage now seemed set for a rough presidential election in 1960.

During my first eighteen months in Korea, UNCURK observed a number of parliamentary by-elections or re-elections. Our normal practice was that one of the members of the Commission, accompanied by an interpreter and a driver, would travel in an UNCURK four-wheel drive vehicle to the electorate. When we approached the site of the election, we would often pick up pedestrians and ask them what they thought of the arrangements being made for the election. We would then interview the candidates and the electoral officials and, on the day of the election, watch the voting, entering the voting stations if permitted, and, at night, watch the counting, what is known in Australia as scrutineering.

Counting of votes had had a tumultuous history in Korea and various malpractices had acquired appropriate names. "Piano voting" referred, for example, to the practice of party officials making appropriate red marks on ballot papers with the tips of their fingers as if they were playing the piano. Thus, ten faked ballots could be marked in the time usually taken to mark one. "Owl-counting" referred to the situation that hapless election officials found themselves in when, if counting had gone against government candidates, party or government officials would disconnect the electricity supply. In the confusion, the latter were able to stuff the boxes full of ballots that had been marked by "piano voting".

During 1958-59, before the presidential and vice-presidential elections of 1960, most of the by-elections we observed were conducted fairly. They took place in rural areas, where support for the Government was strong and the success of its candidates could almost be taken for granted. The opposition (the Democratic Party) was more popular in the cities.

As the presidential elections of 1960 approached, however, changes in the conduct of elections became noticeable. The first oddity was the announcement that the presidential and vice-presidential elections would be held on 15 March 1960. As inauguration of the new President was not due to take place until 15 August 1960, this date seemed unnecessarily early. The reason seemed to be that the Government wanted to get the election out of the way and get the people to accept the result before the inauguration took place. The opposition claimed that its ability to campaign effectively was severely hampered by the inevitably short election campaign.

The eminence grise in the President's office was a certain Mr Kwak, Rhee's chief of staff. I never met Kwak nor anybody else who had met him. Thousands trembled at the mere mention of his name. Years later, when I was in Jordan, Mr Kwak, who had spent some time in prison after the 1960 revolution, turned up there as the representative of one of the big Korean companies. He seemed a most amiable man who belied his sinister reputation.

One of the Government's problems was its candidate for Vice-President. There was no doubt that Syngman Rhee would be the candidate for President. But, as he was already 85, it was questionable whether he would live to serve his full four-year term. The vice-presidential candidate, who would succeed him if he died in office, was the Speaker of the House of Representatives, Lee Ki-poong. Lee Ki-poong had been defeated in the vice-presidential election in 1956 by Dr John M. Chang and Rhee was determined that this would not happen again.

Relations between Lee Ki-poong and the Rhee family were unusually close – so close, in fact, that Syngman Rhee and his wife had adopted Lee Ki-poong's son, Kang-suk, at this time about 20. Lee Ki-poong had a good reputation as a capable politician, and an advocate and practitioner of "clean government." Though not admitted at the time, the problem with him was that he was suffering from an advanced case of syphilis. He was rarely seen in public and no longer presided over the House. Rumours abounded as to exactly what was wrong with him. Several weeks before the 1960 election, the new Australian Representative to UNCURK, John Melhuish, and I called on him. By that stage Lee Ki-poong was unable to stand and had to be brought into his office supported by two muscular secretaries. When tea was served, we noticed that he was unable to lift his cup.

One of the Delegation's confidants, and a source of sound advice during those bizarre days, was Marshall Green, Counsellor in the American Embassy in Seoul, and later American Ambassador to Australia. Green was author of outrageous puns; the one I remember from those days was, "You can't sail the ship of State with a Lee Ki-poong."

Before Lee Ki-Poong's health deteriorated further it was therefore necessary, from the Government's point of view, to get the election over with and to ensure that the Government's candidates won.

It became obvious in some of the by-elections we observed closer to the presidential election that the Government was preparing a massive election fraud. Voters were lined up outside the voting booth and admitted in groups of three. They then entered the booth, marked their ballot papers for the Government and then showed and told each other what they had done, before putting the ballot papers in the box.

There was not much difference between the two parties, politically speaking. Rhee's Liberal Party was, if anything, somewhat more to the left than the opposition Democratic Party and was more popular with poor farmers and fishermen. The Democratic Party relied for support on the city vote and also on Catholics (Vice-President John M. Chang was a Catholic). Both parties actively sought the support of business groups and there had been nothing resembling a left-wing party since the execution of Cho Bong-am of the Progressive Party.

Apart from Rhee, the only other candidate for the presidency was Dr Chough Byong-ok, leader of the Democratic Party's "old faction". The incumbent, Dr John M. Chang from the party's "new faction", was again candidate for Vice-President. There were two other candidates from minor parties for the vice-presidency.

Fate intervened again, as it had in 1956, and Dr Chough died, unexpectedly, in the United States where he had undergone an operation on 15 February 1960, one month before election day. His name appeared on the ballot paper in accordance with the law, but votes for him were regarded as invalid and not included in official tabulations.

The electoral contest, in the absence of any opposition candidate for president, again, as in 1956, became one for the vice-presidency, particularly between Dr Chang Myun and Lee Ki-poong. Dr Chang campaigned vigorously throughout the country. Lee Ki-poong was too ill to campaign. The Liberal Party organisation worked on his behalf. The two other candidates from small parties for the vice-presidency had no chance of success.

Not unexpectedly, it was announced that Syngman Rhee had been re-elected President (9,633,376 votes), and Lee Ki-poong elected Vice-President (8,337,059 votes as against Dr Chang's 1,943,758).

UNCURK had five observer teams in the field. These teams inspected voting stations and interviewed election officials, party workers and private citizens in Seoul and the provinces of Kyunggi Do, Choongchung Namdo, Cholla Pukdo, Cholla Namdo, Kyungsang Pukdo, Kyungsang Namdo and Kangwon Do. We saw what we had seen in the run-up by-elections several months previously – massive rigging and suppression of the opposition vote. In its 1960 report to the General Assembly, UNCURK stated that:

> in the Commission's view, the arrangements for and the conduct of the elections were very far from satisfactory. The observer teams heard many allegations of irregularities and malpractices and themselves noted clear violations of the established voting procedures which caused the Commission serious concern, and of which officials of the Government of the Republic of Korea were apprised following the elections.

There were marked expressions of public discontent about the Government's handling of preparations for the elections. The independent and opposition press were extremely critical and there were a number of demonstrations throughout the country by high school and college students. These demonstrations continued and grew in strength after election day.

The first of the big demonstrations occurred in Masan, a port in the southern province of Kyungsang Namdo, on 15 March (election day). For the first time, police fired on the demonstrators, killing some students and wounding many others. Several people were missing the next day and, on 11 April, the body of one, a fifteen-year old boy, was found, badly mutilated, floating in the harbour of Masan. The population was outraged by this discovery and demonstrations continued in Masan for several days.

At about this time, UNCURK sent me to Tokyo to report on the situation to the three members of the Commission resident in Tokyo – the ambassadors of Chile, Pakistan and the Netherlands. The Ambassador of Chile, Suarez Barros, an elderly man, had been in Japan for many years and took great pride in the collection of rice wine glasses he had amassed as a result of his attendance at New Year's Day and other functions at the Imperial Palace. The Pakistani Ambassador, Mohammed Ali, had been at one stage Prime Minister of Pakistan (one of the few who came from East Pakistan – he was a Bengali). The Dutch Ambassador, de Voogd, had been Counsellor about ten years previously in Canberra when I had been at University with his two sons.

I explained to the ambassadors that the situation in Korea was serious and might deteriorate and urged them to take note of it in the expectation that they might have to visit Korea if UNCURK should have to examine the situation in more detail or take a more active role. Unless the situation improved by Presidential Inauguration Day (15 August), UNCURK would have to be very critical about the Government of Korea in its annual report to the General Assembly. As I was only 26 at that time, I was accompanied on these calls by Keith Brennan, the Counsellor in the Australian Embassy in Tokyo, to add a touch of experience and authority to what I said.

The three ambassadors received my representations well enough, but an unexpected difficulty was the arrival in Tokyo, on their way to Korea, of the two new representatives on UNCURK from the Philippines and Turkey. The Filipino did not seem to have a grasp of the situation and to have some agenda of his own which never became clear. The Turkish Representative had been sent by the repressive government of Menderes, then on its last legs, and had clearly come with instructions to ensure that the UNCURK Report "whitewashed" the situation in Korea. Neither of these accepted my version of events and it became even clearer when they arrived in Seoul that they would add new and disruptive elements to UNCURK proceedings. Our meetings became evermore turbulent, but were eventually overtaken by events and the Filipino and the Turk had to abandon their stance when, about a month after their arrival, the Korean Government fell (the Menderes Government in Turkey fell some time later).

While in Tokyo, I had dinner with the Head of the Korean Mission in Japan, Yiu Tae-ha. President Rhee had always refused to enter into diplomatic relations with Japan or to accept Japanese Representation in Korea. Some contact, however, was necessary and Korea maintained a diplomatic mission in Japan headed by a senior figure. Yiu Tae-ha was a legendary and greatly feared figure in the Korean Foreign Service who, I think, had once been Foreign Minister. I had heard endless tales about his fearsome and ruthless personality, his horrible treatment of subordinates and his immense collection of white shirts. His deputy in Japan, whom I had known in the Foreign Ministry in Seoul, told me that Ambassador Yiu had been instructed to take me out to dinner and find out what I was doing in Tokyo. After having accepted the invitation, I was informed by this official that under no circumstances was I to fail to turn up at the dinner; his own life would not be worth living if Ambassador Yiu came to the venue and I was not there.

The dinner eventually took place in a Japanese restaurant

where, as I recall, the three of us – Yiu Tae-ha, the official and myself, sat on the floor. I could well believe that all I had heard about Yiu Tae-ha was true, but I can only report that he treated me very well, and with great courtesy. When he asked me why I was in Tokyo, I said I was there to discuss the Korean election with my Tokyo colleagues. When he asked what I had said, I replied that I did not want to spoil the evening with a recitation of such unpleasant events. Yiu Tae-ha had to remain satisfied with that account.

As if that were not enough, I was mixed up in a most embarrassing episode, largely of my own making, which caused some embarrassment with the Korean Foreign Ministry. As I was leaving the airport to fly to Japan, a Korean journalist friend asked me if I would take an envelope with me to a friend of his in Japan. I had had no experience with this sort of thing before and, without thinking, took the envelope and put it in my pocket. As I went through customs, I was asked, politely enough, whether anyone had given me anything for anybody in Japan. I at once handed over the envelope which, I later learned, contained visas for foreign journalists to enter Korea to cover the post-election situation. After the visas had been issued, the Government had had second thoughts and the order had gone out to retrieve them. They had been planted on me by those wanting the journalists to come to Korea, but the police had observed the encounter.

As I sat in the plane wondering what the consequences of all this would be, I remembered that I had been given a second, much smaller, envelope which was still in my coat pocket; in the haste of the moment, I had forgotten to hand it over. I examined it and found to my horror that it was a cheque for US $5,000 on an American bank for a senior Korean newspaper magnate then in Japan. What would have been the consequences if I had been found with that, I could not and did not want to imagine. Mere possession of the cheque violated every known currency law in Korean.

When I arrived in Tokyo, I saw no point in handing over the cheque to the Japanese customs. They would have been almost as embarrassed to receive it as I was. I stayed with some Australians at the Embassy in Tokyo and discussed the matter with them. We finally came to the conclusion that, as I had passed through both the Korean and Japanese customs without the cheque having been discovered, I might as well hand it over to its rightful owner. I therefore called him and, later that night, had a somewhat sinister assignation in the shrubbery of my hosts' grounds, where I gave him the cheque.

I reported this the next day to John Melhuish, my boss in Seoul, who took up the matter of the visas with the Korean Foreign Ministry. The Ministry was surprisingly relaxed about the whole episode. Possibly the official sensed that the Government's days were numbered; possibly he even sympathised with the plan to get the journalists into the country. In any case, there were no unpleasant repercussions. The Department of External Affairs in Canberra, to which we also reported the episode, was considerably more concerned.

Until 18 April, Seoul itself, despite demonstrations in Masan and elsewhere, had remained comparatively calm. On the evening of 18 April, however, a number of students from one of Korea's leading universities gathered in front of the National Assembly protesting against the elections. The group later dispersed but, on their way home, some of its members were set upon by hoodlums who attacked and injured many of them with knives, bicycle chains and other weapons. The violence against the students was popularly believed to have been instigated by people close to the Government.

The next day, large numbers of students from many of Seoul's universities gathered on the road leading to the President's residence and protested against the election and against the attack on the university students the night before. Police fired on these demonstrators, killing or wounding hundreds.

Medical students (white coats) assisting wounded demonstrators during the revolution of 19 April 1960

The UNCURK office was near the road leading to the Presidential mansion and I was able to witness and photograph the scenes described above. Koreans I have spoken to since have told me that there are comparatively few photographs of the events of that day – they occurred too quickly for people to witness them. My photographs are very dramatic. Some show the students crouching on the road as the police fired. Others show the wounded being tended by medical students, who wore white coats to identify them. When I was in Bangladesh many years later, I showed the photographs to the new Korean Ambassador. He scrutinised one in particular – showing a group of students setting fire to a police station – and explained that he had been one of those participating.

Later the same day, 19 April, President Rhee proclaimed Martial Law in five major cities – Seoul, Pusan, Taegu, Taejon, and Kwangju. Rhee undoubtedly expected that the army would suppress the students and maintain him in power. The Martial Law Commander, General Song Yo-chan (Army Chief of Staff), however, adopted an unexpectedly conciliatory attitude, arrested some of the hoodlums who had attacked the students on 18 April, and interviewed and praised the students. In these circumstances, the city remained calm and attention focussed on President Rhee and his Cabinet.

This took Rhee by surprise. He issued several statements in which he offered to sever all connection with the Liberal Party, and to investigate all major grievances when the situation had returned to normal. The demonstrators did not consider these statements sufficient concessions. On the evening of 25 April, a group of professors from major universities in Seoul gathered and was quickly joined by tens of thousands of students and other persons in demonstrations which continued well into the next day. The army remained aloof.

For several days before this, I had been living in the UNCURK Castle to be near our files and communications material in case of a major breakdown in law and order. On the afternoon of 25 April (after a somewhat disturbed ANZAC Day ceremony in the morning), as things seemed quiet, and needing some fresh clothes, I set out in the car to my apartment at the other end of town. On the way, I met the procession of professors. Knowing that demonstrations had been banned, I realised that this meant trouble. I returned to the UNCURK Castle immediately.

That night I heard what sounded like massive gunfire going on throughout the city and saw flares, searchlights and other indications of violent activity. In an action that would be criminal to-day under the Freedom of Information Act (and no doubt other legislation), I burnt all the delegation's files going back to 1950 in the UNCURK oil heating fire-system. Why this did not burn down the entire building I am now not sure, but at the time I did not even think about that possibility. The next day it turned out that what I had heard and seen did not amount to a major fight between the army and the population but were the sounds of blanks being fired and similar events.

On 26 April, the police were now discredited because of their firing on the students on 19 April, the army was neutral and a large proportion of the population of Seoul was demonstrating against the Government. Rhee consequently found his situation increasingly difficult to maintain. Later that day he announced he was willing, should the people wish it, to resign and call fresh elections. The National Assembly, acting as representative of the people (the Vice-President, Dr Chang, had resigned on 23 April), accepted the President's decision that day.

The next day, 27 April, ex-President Rhee drove from his Presidential mansion through the city to a small house where he went into exile. I was standing on the main street on which he passed after leaving his residence. The streets were crowded on both sides with people who pressed forward to cheer the ex-President and wish him well in his exile. They did not want him back, but were expressing their appreciation for his role as the Father of his country and making it clear that they would not support any vindictive actions against him personally for what had recently occurred. Rhee sat in his car, blinking in confusion and gently acknowledging the crowd's farewell. Shortly after, he left for permanent exile in Hawaii.

It was interesting to experience a revolution in my first post. The only other revolution I went through was in my last post, thirty years later, in Bangladesh, when President Ershad was driven from office in a surprisingly similar manifestation of people power. These revolutions led me to the conclusion that it is not true that Asians do not want democracy. Authoritarian governments may last for some time, but they cannot survive if they insult their people or are manifestly venal and corrupt. Rhee could have easily been elected again if he had not tried to impose the syphilitic Lee Ki-poong on the electorate. The latter came to a sad end. Several days later, his son, Lee Kang-suk, who had been adopted by President Rhee and his wife, shot Lee Ki-poong, Mrs Lee Ki-poong and their only other son, and then shot himself. I was told that the crowds demanded to see the bodies so they could be assured that Lee Ki-poong was really dead.

There was a palpable feeling of relief when the old order was overthrown. For weeks, either because of the cold or because of the volatile political situation, everybody had been forced to stay at home or in the office. Tempers were frayed; nobody had had any idea how long the crisis would last or what the outcome would be. Many had expected the army to take the side of the President and seek to suppress the people. The sudden fall of the Government coincided with the onset of spring and it was a great relief to be able to get out and move around again in the countryside.

Under the Constitution, the Foreign Minister, Mr Huh Chung, who had been appointed to this office several days before Dr Rhee's resignation, became Acting President. Mr Huh had no post in the administration at the time of the revolution, although he had held several important positions earlier including that of the Mayor of Seoul. He immediately pledged that his administration would hold National Assembly elections in July 1960 and would work with the National Assembly to pass a constitutional amendment replacing the existing presidential system with a system of cabinet government.

Like many people in countries without much experience in democracy, Koreans in those days believed that the political turmoil their country had gone through was due, at least in part, to their having chosen the wrong type of government. They thought that the presidential system gave the President too much power at the expense of the Parliament and that a reduction in presidential powers would lead to more balanced government. This proved a mistaken view, in Korea and in other countries. The real problem was the attitudes of the Government, the opposition and the people themselves.

The constitutional amendments duly passed by the National Assembly (which still had a Liberal Party majority) in June

1960 provided for a parliamentary system, with the president, as head of state, to be elected by members of both houses at a joint session. Executive powers were vested in a prime minister who was nominated by the president and approved by the House of Representatives.

Elections for the new National Assembly were held on 29 July 1960. The Liberal Party of President Rhee had virtually disappeared by this time and the Democratic Party (of Dr John M. Chang, the former Vice-President) remained the only major party to contest the election. The elections were a victory for the Democratic Party which won 175 of the 233 seats contested. UNCURK observed these elections and noted, in its 1960 report to the General Assembly, that "arrangements for and the conduct of the elections were very satisfactory."

As a result of these elections, Dr Chang became the new prime minister with executive power. The new president, now almost purely a head of state figure, was Yun Po-sun, a member of Cho Byong-ok's faction. He had been educated at Edinburgh University.

There was a genuine sense of achievement in Korea when the new Government was formed. At the beginning of 1960, it seemed that there was little alternative to another four years of Syngman Rhee. But, whatever his past achievements, he was by then manifestly too old to be an effective leader. Lee Ki-poong, paralysed almost completely, was a most inappropriate heir apparent. Most believed that the army was too loyal to oppose Rhee in any way. When, as a result of the students' initiative, the army yielded to the people and the old system was swept aside, the Koreans, and the foreigners in their midst, felt they had really accomplished something unexpected that gave them a new sense of confidence.

There were nevertheless doubts about the new leadership. Dr Chang Myun had never been an effective figure, even as Vice-

President. It was not certain that he could handle the rough and tumble of Korean politics. Yun Po-sun, a respected member of the upper class, had shown little capacity for leadership. These misgivings were vindicated when, in April 1961, Dr Chang was swept from office after a military coup led by General Park Chung-hi and Korea went down a different path. General Park, in the event, was shot dead in the late 1970s at a dinner party which he himself was hosting.

It would be nice to say that throughout these tumultuous proceedings, the Australian Delegation to UNCURK had received full and timely guidance from the Department of External Affairs in Canberra about how to conduct itself. As is often the case, however, everyone seemed to be about two beats behind what was actually happening. Although the Australian Government and the Department knew of the importance of Korea in a strategic sense, it had not expected and did not want it to heat up politically so quickly. The Government's attention was directed towards other areas – Laos, the Straits of Taiwan, Vietnam (even in those days). The Department had already been through the presidential election of 1956 and saw no reason why the 1960 election should be much different. Indeed, it had given every promise of being almost identical, particularly when the leading challenger died during the campaign.

All through 1959 we were unable to persuade the Department to realise the seriousness of the situation in Korea and the crisis that might eventually erupt. The Department rejected our draft of the political chapter of the UNCURK Report for that year on the grounds that it was too critical of the Korean Government and insisted that we draft another, more anodyne version.

In retrospect, the key problem was the illness of Lee Ki-poong. The extent of his incapacity had been kept secret for some time, although it was known that he was too ill to preside over sessions of the National Assembly. The seriousness of the situation did not really hit us until after the 15 March election when, in view of the obvious rigging, we began to doubt whether Lee Ki-poong would actually take his seat as Vice-President on Inauguration Day, 15 August. But we could not imagine exactly what would happen to prevent his doing so. That particular question was answered much more quickly than we had expected.

One bizarre episode took place one month before I left Korea late in 1960 when a group of Australian parliamentarians arrived on a visit. One morning I was awakened early by a call from Jenny Melhuish, the wife the then Australian Representative to UNCURK, asking me to come to their house immediately as one of the parliamentarians, Frank Timson, a Liberal from Victoria, had died during the night. This was completely unexpected and we had no contingency plans.

First, we had to arrange an appropriate funeral. As I recall it, the then Korean Foreign Minister was a Christian and he organised a dignified ceremony in his own local parish church. One unexpected problem was that we did not have the obligatory (in Korea) photograph of the deceased to put on the altar. Fortunately, the previous evening, we had held a reception at which the deceased MP had been photographed, smiling and holding a glass of whisky. We very carefully removed the latter from the photograph and had it enlarged. The result proved entirely fitting for the purpose for which it was needed. The funeral went very well and we were all, including the Foreign Minister, photographed standing next to the hearse.

Next we had to decide what to do with the body. The member's relatives wanted it returned to Australia but there was no obvious way of transporting it. Fortunately, as so often happened in Korea, the American Embassy and army came to the rescue. They had any number of coffins of all shapes and sizes and even a special plane on which to fly it out. A suitable coffin was found and we all went down to the American air base to farewell it. The plane roared to the end of the runway and then stopped; some mishap in the engine made take off impossible. I burst into spontaneous applause at this particular point and was sharply reprimanded by John Melhuish. Fortunately, another plane was found and the episode came to a satisfactory, if sad, end.

Korea was an excellent introduction to Asia. The Koreans, as I later found the Burmese, easily became friends. Each Korean seemed to have individual characteristics which set him or her off from other Koreans. (I cannot say I have found the same to be true of all other nationalities.) Politically it was probably the most interesting post I ever had and, in those days, it was a really foreign country, as different from Australia as it possibly could be. The countryside was beautiful and well worth travelling in. The comfortable Korean inns with their heated wax-paper floors and Chinese dinners were ideal resting places. Korean painting, sculpture, bronze work and, above all, celadon, have a special quality all their own and, fortunately, it was still possible while I was there to buy beautiful examples of them at relatively low prices. Some are now on display in the Queensland Art Gallery. The beautiful, old Buddhist temples in remote, mountainous parts of the country repaid a visit..

One Korean practice I did not like was that of putting a raw egg into a cup of coffee. I had to make sure not to stir the coffee and thus adulterating it. Years later, I mentioned this to the Korean Ambassador in Jordan. He laughed and said this habit had lasted for only the two years I was in Korea and had long since been abandoned.

No one in Korea in 1960 would have believed that Korea would make the economic progress that it has since made. This was not only because the Government then might have chosen the wrong economic policy (for example, not allowing Japanese investment in Korea). Most foreigners, and possibly even the Koreans themselves, did not think that Koreans were capable of making much progress. They were not as "clever" as the Chinese or as well organised – or as capable of being as well-organised – as the Japanese. This was not an attitude held by Westerners only; both the Chinese and the Japanese were thought to despise the Koreans. (Even now, I have found remnants of this attitude in some Arab countries where the Koreans have undertaken construction work.)

Part of the problem was thought to be that the Koreans lacked a satisfactory national ethos. Most Koreans held Confucian ideals, if only sub-consciously, but no Korean would have seriously described himself as Confucian. Buddhism, after an initial high-water mark centuries ago, had become disengaged from modern life and had fled to temple retreats in the mountains. The old Korean feudal system and the court that went with it had been totally discredited. Probably the Christians were the most motivated religious group, particularly Catholics, but there were simply not enough for Korea ever to become a Christian country. It was believed that this lack of a national ethos meant that the Koreans were insufficiently disciplined to make economic progress.

Korea had few natural resources. Korea was agriculturally rich, but all the mineral deposits were thought to be in North Korea which also had good hydro-power facilities. When asked where they thought their economic future lay, most Korean officials would look blank and, as mentioned above, suggest that fruits, nuts and seaweed were about all they had to export.

In retrospect, one can see that there were resources that could be exploited, the most important being labour (the population in the south was then 22 million). There was also a great thirst for education and a tenacious will to succeed; the literacy rate was therefore high. But it is true to say that the Koreans had given little hint in those days that they had the organisational capacity required to build on these resources and to create a great economy. That they were able to develop this capacity must be one of the real success stories of modern times.

I was surprised when I returned to Korea for a brief holiday in 1990 during my posting in Bangladesh, just before President Ershad fell from power. Much of the Seoul I knew had vanished, except for the part in the middle of town which was much the same. What struck me most, however, was how much less English seemed to be spoken than when I had been there thirty years earlier.

In those days, Koreans of all kinds had been very much influenced by the war – in particular, by the presence of thousands of American troops from whom they, drivers, waiters, servants, and soldiers, had learned some English. The leadership then, for the most part, had spent many years in exile where they had used English (and, in some cases, other languages) constantly. Thus, some English was spoken at all levels of society and it was comparatively easy to conduct official business.

By 1990, however, it was very different. The waiters and concierges in the hotels in Seoul understood English only with difficulty and, outside Seoul, not at all. It was difficult to find anyone who spoke English in shops. After a few days of this, it occurred to me that, in recent years, very few of the Korean ambassadors with whom I had served had spoken English as well as Foreign Ministry officials had when I was in Seoul.

3
ISRAEL, 1963-65
Changing Attitudes

When I returned to the Department after Korea, I worked for a year on East Asian affairs and was later, for another year, the editor of *Current Notes on International Affairs*, the Department's publication. I was then posted to Israel where I arrived on 2 June 1963, exactly five years after I had arrived in Korea.

Reaching Israel proved even more complicated than reaching Seoul. I flew first to Hong Kong (again to get suits made), but developed an abscess in one tooth that had to be removed when I reached Hong Kong; the drop in pressure in the plane had encouraged the abscess to develop. This weakened my system considerably so I had to delay my departure while I recovered in the hotel. There was a water shortage, and I had to pour water out of a bucket into the bath whenever I wanted to wash myself, a difficult task in view of my condition.

After recovery, I flew to New Delhi, mainly to meet a friend from the American Embassy in Seoul who was now stationed in India. We had both attended the same primary school in New York, at different times, and that always gave us something to talk about. After several days there, I flew to Tehran on BOAC. There, the plane developed some technical fault and we could not leave Tehran for three or four days. The airline accommodated us in a hotel, but we did not see much of the city. The hotel had an elevator which bore a sign, "Before entering the elevator, make sure it is there". This did not inspire confidence in the hotel or Tehran. Tehran was the first Middle Eastern city I had seen and I thought it was drab and uninteresting.

I therefore arrived in Tel Aviv about a week after I had planned to. The Embassy had arranged a welcome party for me which had to go ahead without me. I sensed that the entire episode had given the Embassy a feeling that I was unreliable.

Although Korea had been an exciting and exotic post, it was a fairly straightforward and "normal" Asian posting for the 1950s. Israel was something quite different, a unique country which seemed in some ways even more foreign than Korea. Its major pre-occupation, the Arab-Israel dispute, was something with which I was to have much to do for the next 25 years.

In 1922, the League of Nations had mandated the territory of Palestine, part of the Ottoman Empire for centuries, to the British to administer until such time as it was able to stand alone. At that time, the area was inhabited largely by Arabs. The British Government, however, in the Balfour Declaration of 1917, had declared that it favoured the establishment of a Jewish National Home in Palestine. Subsequent Jewish immigration to Palestine led to conflict and disagreement between Jews and Arabs which proved irreconcilable.

The United Nations General Assembly, in Resolution 181 (111) of 29 November 1947, called for partition of Palestine into Arab and Jewish states with the city of Jerusalem as a *corpus separatum* to be governed by an international regime. The Resolution, considered by the Jewish community in Palestine to be a legal basis for the establishment of Israel, was rejected by the Arab community and was succeeded almost immediately by violence between the Arab and Jewish communities. Forces from the adjoining Arab states also intervened.

On 15 May 1948, the day that the last British forces left what had been the Mandated Territory of Palestine, David Ben-Gurion, the Jewish leader, proclaimed the State of Israel. It was immediately recognised by the United States and the Soviet Union. The Arab states then marched into Israel, starting the first Arab-Israeli War.

Armistice Agreements were signed with Egypt, Lebanon, Jordan and Syria in 1949. Israel held much of the territory it had been allocated by the United Nations except for the area to the west of the Jordan River that became known as the "West Bank", and was held by Jordan. Jerusalem remained divided between Jordan and Israel but, in 1949, Ben-Gurion, now Prime Minister, declared it to be the capital of Israel.

Border skirmishes occurred frequently in the following years, but the first real crisis was in 1956 when, following nationalisation of the Suez Canal by Egypt, Israeli, British and French forces attacked Egypt in an attempt to wrest control of the Canal from Egypt. This effort failed, largely because of the opposition of the United States. Israel, however, did occupy the Sinai desert. Upon receiving United States guarantees of Israeli access to the Gulf of Aqaba, the Israelis withdrew to the Negev desert in Israel. At Egypt's request, the United Nations sent an Emergency Force (UNEF) consisting of 6,000 peacekeeping troops from ten nations to supervise the ceasefire. It was withdrawal of this force and the consequent closure of the Gulf of Aqaba to Israel that caused the Arab-Israeli War in 1967. At the United Nations General Assembly's deliberations of the Suez crisis in 1956, Australia, along with New Zealand, supported the French-British-Israeli position, largely at the insistence of the Prime Minister, R. G. Menzies.

By the time I arrived in 1963, Israel had become one of the great success stories of the era. Its leaders knew what they wanted and how to achieve it. Between 1950 and 1965, real GNP grew by an average annual rate of more than 11 per cent and per capita GNP by more than 6 per cent. This was made possible by large capital inflows, such as German reparations and restitutions, the sale of Israel Bonds, and loans from the United States. The population was slightly more than two million, about 15 per cent of whom were Arabs. Between 1948 and 1962, Israel had absorbed nearly one million migrants, a colossal undertaking for a new state. Import substitution was encouraged by government budgets and strong protectionist measures. These aided development of new industries such as textiles and old industries such as citrus products and cut diamonds. The crime rate was low.

My first Ambassador in Tel Aviv was Mr John D. L. Hood, already a legendary and controversial figure in the Australian diplomatic service who had been in the Department since its

Ambassador and Mrs J. D. L. Hood in their garden in Tel Aviv

creation before the war. Before I left Canberra, senior officials who posted me to Israel told me that Mr Hood (I still think of him in those terms) was the ablest and most perspicacious officer ever to work in the Department. I never saw any reason to dispute this.

Hood had been a Rhodes Scholar from Tasmania recruited immediately on graduation from Oxford as a leader writer at the London *Times*. He joined the Australian Department of External Affairs in 1935 and attended many important international conferences, including that in 1945 which established the United Nations; he was President of the Security Council in 1947. He had also been at the Nuremberg War Crimes trials. Later he became Australian Ambassador to Indonesia and, subsequently, to the Federal Republic of Germany.

Hood was the Australian member of the United Nations Special Commission on Palestine (UNSCOP) which was established in May 1947 and whose report led to Resolution 181 (III) of 20 November 1947 leading to the creation of Israel. During its deliberations, UNSCOP had visited Palestine where its members got to know the Jewish and Arab leaders. Hood told me that, when he was a member of UNSCOP, he had not been convinced by the Jewish case. The Minister for External Affairs, Dr H. V. Evatt, a convinced Zionist, had, however, instructed him that he was not to do anything that would prevent creation of a Jewish State in Palestine. He did not tell me what he would have done if he had not received this instruction. In any case, the UNSCOP recommendation that Palestine be partitioned was adopted.

Whether or not they knew of his doubts about creation of Israel, Hood was very well remembered by senior Israeli ministers such as Moshe Sharrett, Abba Eban and Golda Meir and was the only person I ever saw them defer to. His intelligence and manner had made a great impression on them and they spoke of him almost with awe. He is the only Australian diplomat, as far as I know, whose retirement was news on the front page of the London

Times. People to-day (whose retirements were not reported in that journal) may sneer at this fact, but it was an indication of how highly he was regarded in international circles, particularly at the United Nations.

It is, however, not revealing any secret to say that after his posting to Indonesia he had begun to drink so much that he could not be depended on to be sober on those occasions when sobriety in an ambassador was essential. A remark he made to me once – "when I emerge from a restaurant after lunch, I expect it to be dark outside" – gave some indication of his preferred lifestyle. After his posting to Germany, it was difficult to post him anywhere as Head of Mission and the Department of External Affairs gave him a number of lesser jobs, including Deputy Permanent Representative at the United Nations in the early 1960s. By the time he was approaching sixty (1964), the department wanted him to retire as an Ambassador and posted him to Israel where he served a year before retirement. The Israelis were pleased with the appointment and there were no serious problems about drinking during that period. I was his deputy virtually for the whole time he was there.

What impressed me most about him was his judgment. Many of the people I have worked with have had some particular quirk or dislike which clouded their ability to assess events clearly. They want to blame, for example, the Americans, or the French, or even the New Zealanders, for anything that goes wrong. Mr Hood had no such prejudices and a keen intuition enabled him to weigh all the factors in any situation very clearly and dispassionately. He, and Sir Walter Crocker, another Head of Mission with whom I served, were the best stylists, as writers, that I ever knew in the Department and, like Sir Walter, Mr Hood was not a tiresome pedant about grammar. Nor did he have any pre-occupations about his own status as a Head of Mission. Apart from his drinking, he commanded respect naturally and did not have to demand it. His manners were perfect and he was always considerate to staff. Like Sir Walter, he had a great gift for setting people at their ease.

Shortly before Hood left Israel, Golda Meir, then Foreign Minister, gave a farewell lunch for him. The conversation turned to a recent film, *Cast a Giant Shadow*, in which Kirk Douglas played the part of the Jewish West Point graduate, Mickey Marcus, who had joined the Israeli Army and fought in the War of Independence in 1948-49. Hood, feeling rather morose that day, probably because he was leaving the service after many years of ups and downs, was not paying much attention to what was being said. But he suddenly burst forth with, "But, Mme Minister, what's Mickey Mouse got to do with the War of Independence?" Mme Minister explained the conversation was about Mickey Marcus, not Mickey Mouse; but the seriousness of the discussion had been irreparably impaired.

Sir Paul Hasluck, in *Diplomatic Witness*, makes ten references to Hood, all unfavourable. Dame Alexandra Hasluck makes equally deprecatory references in *Portrait in a Mirror*, her autobiography, to the first Mrs Hood. There was, evidently, some deep antipathy between them dating from the war and the postwar years in the Department of External Affairs in Canberra. Sir Paul became Minister for External Affairs shortly before Mr Hood retired and the latter told me that, had he not been about to retire, he would have resigned because he would not work for Hasluck whom he described as a "fascist", although regretting that he had to use such a word about an Australian. I never heard him speak in such terms about anyone else.

I felt that many of Hood's' problems had been caused by the fact that he had entered the wrong profession. Although suited to diplomacy in many ways, he probably would have been happier in a more settled job, in a stable environment in a university or on a newspaper. He seemed stressed by the peripatetic demands of diplomatic life. In addition, although an intellectual and a person of vast experience who had seen much and remembered what he had seen, he had no real intellectual interests and seemed to prefer to read crime stories to anything else. He lacked an all-embracing interest that would have given a focus to his life.

In any case, after retirement, he lived happily in France, outliving many of his more sober contemporaries and dying at about the age of 88.

After Hood retired, I was charge d'affaires for nearly a year until the arrival of the next ambassador, Mr W. G. A. Landale. Landale came from a wealthy Victorian pastoral family and had very strong opinions about behaviour and protocol. He told me once that one could only ever wear a sweater without a coat if one were mustering or yachting. As I never mustered or yachted, this advice was not of much use.

This was my first experience at being in charge of an overseas mission. It was a stimulating time because it coincided with the first indications, such as establishment of the Palestine Liberation Organization (PLO), of the troubles that would lead to the Six Day War in 1967. Despite these forebodings, the years I was in Israel, 1963-65, must seem to many Israelis who remember them as having been the country's golden age. Israel was firmly established on the international scene, assimilation of migrants had proceeded well, the army was strong and confident, economic development had proved possible, a national identity had been established, and Hebrew had taken root as the national language. Most Israelis were satisfied with their borders, although some undoubtedly would have liked to expand to the West Bank or at least to East Jerusalem. On the whole, however, the country seemed to be looking forward to a period of peace and development.

Life in Israel at that time had some curious features. It is hard to realise now that I arrived there only fifteen years after its establishment. Many Israelis seemed to be still getting used to the idea of having a state. Almost all the Israelis the Embassy knew seemed to know one another and had played various roles in the independence movement, as lawyers, members of the Jewish army in the Independence War or as apologists for the cause. Tel Aviv itself had a small-town, informal atmosphere and, at the same time, an air of intense vitality. The country seemed really on the move.

Life amongst the diplomatic community was close partly because most of us felt we were in a very foreign country and we needed mutual support. Because strategic considerations were important and we did not have a services attaché, I formed a useful relationship with the Canadian air attaché. The American Embassy officers were also useful sources of information as they kept their ears very close to the ground. We saw a lot of the British Embassy, located across the street, mainly because of the Commonwealth connection and because we might have to rely on them in case of emergency evacuation. I was surprised, therefore, when I called on the Embassy to discuss this point, the relevant official read from a document from London that "you should not be drawn into discussions with the Australians about what arrangements might be made in case of an emergency".

Travelling in Israel was easy as the roads were good and there were many fascinating archaeological sites to visit, particularly in the north in Galilee where there was still a considerable Arab presence. It was also possible to cross into the Old City of Jerusalem via the Mandelbaum Gate and visit the sites there. In view of what has happened recently, it is interesting to recall that when I used to cross over on Friday afternoon and visit the Dome of the Rock, the great Muslim site was usually completely deserted, except for a few sweepers or caretakers. There was no one praying.

Internal political developments that took place in Israel during this time must seem like ancient history to any present day student of its affairs. The country was very much under the dominance of the Labour Party, or Mapai as it was known. There had only been two prime ministers – David Ben-Gurion (1886-1973) and Moshe Sharrett. Sharrett (1894-1965) had been Prime Minister from January 1954 to November 1955. Ben-Gurion, in his second run as prime minister, resigned in a fit of petulance shortly after I arrived and was succeeded as by Levi Eshkol (1896-1969), a figure who I imagine is almost forgotten to-day.

Menachem Begin (1913-92) and his opposition Herut Party (later Likud) were virtually ostracised not only by the Israeli establishment itself but also by the diplomatic corps. As I recall, Begin was on our "Visa Warning List" which meant that he was not to be issued a visa because of his behaviour towards the British army in Palestine before independence, particularly the bombing of the King David Hotel in Jerusalem in 1946. I do not remember meeting him or hearing anybody else claim to have met him. No one seemed to give him any hope of becoming prime minister. It seemed assumed that Mapai's dominance of Israel would continue forever. Ben-Gurion always used to say that he would form a coalition with anyone except the communists and Herut. The general view of people we met was that both Begin and his party were extremists who should not be entrusted with power. In view of the way he was treated by his own people, and by foreigners, it seems extraordinary that Begin retained, as I am told he did, his respect for formality and protocol behaviour until the day he died.

Relations between Israel and the United States were nothing like they are now. In view of what has happened since, it is worth underlining that United States' first period of economic grants to Israel ended in 1959. United States aid to Israel from then until 1985 consisted largely of loans, which Israel repaid, and surplus commodities, which Israel bought. It did receive plenty of American money through private channels from the sale of Israel Bonds and such like but it received no governmental assistance. Nor was there any pressure for American aid. Israel was perfectly capable of taking care of itself militarily in any confrontation with the Arabs.

What the Israelis would have liked, and what they did not get, was some kind of American guarantee of their borders. Israel began buying arms from the United States in 1962, but did not receive any military assistance from the United States until after the Yom Kippur War in 1973. I have not had occasion to study the history of this matter but it would be very intriguing to know how and why the United States found itself in the position where it is obliged to provide Israel with several billion dollars' worth of military aid every year and even to guarantee Israel's overseas borrowings. This was not necessary in 1963; why is it necessary now?

Australia was well regarded in Israel in the 1960s. Australian soldiers who had served in the Middle East during the Second World War were remembered for their informality and friendliness. There were many anecdotes about their escapades which were thought to be livelier than the more solemn behaviour of the British. The leadership knew not only of Hood's work on the United Nations Commission, but also of Dr Evatt's support at the United Nations for the establishment of Israel. One Israeli diplomat commented publicly once that the creation of Israel owed as much to Dr Evatt as it did to any one man. And, although they did not mention it much, Israelis also remembered the support that we had extended to them, in the face of opposition from many other countries, during the Suez crisis of 1956.

Apart from these considerations, our ties were slight. The only diplomatic posts we had in the Middle East were in Israel and Cairo. Our Mission in Tel Aviv consisted of the Ambassador, myself, an administrative officer, a secretary-archivist, a locally engaged migration clerk, a telephonist, an illiterate cleaner and two drivers. The Ambassador once observed to me that our duties seemed mostly to take care of visitors, most of them Australian

Jews. Many Australian politicians came to Israel to show their support and to impress their Jewish constituents. Prominent Zionists from Australia often appeared as did Australian Jews who had established businesses in Israel. Trade did not amount to much, although some Australian companies had interests in Israel. Pioneer Concrete, for example, established a factory there in the early 1960s.

Among the visitors during my posting were Arthur A. Calwell, then Leader of the Opposition; Henry Bolte, Premier of Victoria; Arthur Rylah, his deputy; and Gough Whitlam, Deputy Leader of the Opposition. Zelman Cowen and his family also visited Israel at the invitation, as I recall, of the Hebrew University in Jerusalem.

The Israelis handled these visits, often made at their initiative, very well. I do not remember to what extent they paid for them. Calwell was travelling at the expense of the Australian Government, but the Israelis usually provided cars and assigned a senior Israeli diplomat as host. The visitor would be given a briefing on Israeli internal and external affairs and taken around the country to see the development taking place. Almost invariably, the visitors returned to Australia with a high regard for Israeli policies and achievements. The Arab countries could well have emulated this pattern of encouraging visitors, but they did not do so. As I later discovered, they were prone to harass visitors on what they felt was the tendency of the West to let them down at every possible opportunity.

On the other hand, some Australian Jews expressed resentment at what they regarded as assumptions by Israel that Jews in the diaspora should support Israel on all occasions and owed Israel some kind of extra-territorial allegiance. One eminent Jewish lawyer from Melbourne told us that he was intending to tell the Prime Minister of Israel that other countries were fed up with having to support the Palestinian refugees and that Israel should

Henry (later Sir Henry) Bolte, Premier of Victoria (standing), former Israeli Prime Minister David Ben-Gurion (white hair) and Richard Gate (white pants) at a ceremony in the Negev Desert, 1964

make a gesture which would settle the problem once and for all. Hood was able to dissuade him from doing so as he knew that the Prime Minister would say that the refugee problem was only part of the larger problem which could not be solved until the Arabs recognised Israel.

One event of potential significance was the planned visit to Israel in 1964 of the then Prime Minister, Sir Robert Menzies. This was an unexpected development; indeed, there seemed to be some reluctance on his part to undertake the visit. His announcement of it noted that he had been for some time "under pressure" to visit Israel. Our resources for coping with such a visit in Tel Aviv were small and, to my surprise, Hood, sensing that our Embassy looked rather thin on the ground, persuaded two Australia-based officers from the High Commission in London to come to Tel Aviv to thicken our ranks. He also wanted to get some well-known Jews with Israeli connexions, and whom Menzies knew, such as Danny Kaye and Isaac Stern, to be in Israel at the time, but this proved impossible. There was a feeling of general relief all around when the visit was cancelled after Sir Robert had been afflicted with diverticulitis.

The Israelis sometimes handled these visits in strange ways. During Whitlam's visit, he was taken to a ceremony in a remote part of the country honouring an important Zionist leader who had just died. The entire proceedings were conducted in Hebrew. The solemn nature of the occasion meant that very little outward emotion was displayed by any of the participants. Whitlam found it impossible to understand anything about the proceedings and left the occasion completely mystified.

It was difficult to find any matters of common political interest between Australia and Israel. In Korea, Australian participation in the Korean War, our role in post-war reconstruction and our membership of UNCURK, with its special interest in domestic politics, gave us reasons to be concerned with events there, a concern which was accepted, however reluctantly, by the Korean Government. Later, when I served in Italy, our common membership of Western alliances (NATO, on the one hand, and ANZUS, on the other) and the flood of Italian migration to Australia gave our governments something to talk about. Again, in Burma, our large aid program and our participation in the annual World Bank aid consortiums about Burma gave us a legitimate reason to engage in a dialogue with the Burmese Government.

These considerations were not present in Israel. In 1963-65, Australia's main foreign policy concern was the Cold War. Israel then, whatever might have been the case later, did not see itself as a supporter of Western interests in the Middle East (nor did we argue that it should). Ben-Gurion had always spoken of "non-identification" with the two power blocs (that is, non-alignment). Israel's entire concern was with the Arab threat, a threat which was in some ways assisted by the Soviet Union. Israel had no interest in antagonising the Soviet Union more than was necessary lest this should add to Soviet support for its Arab enemies. Moreover, Israel was anxious to keep its lines open to the Soviet Union to tap the potential stream of Jews wanting to emigrate from that country. The fact that many of the arms that had enabled the Jews to win the War of Independence had come from Soviet-bloc countries created a bond, however tenuous, with those countries. On one occasion, when I was charge d'affaires, I had to deliver to the Foreign Minister, Golda Meir, a letter from the Minister for External Affairs, Paul Hasluck, the purpose of which was to arouse some sympathy for the American-Australian position in the Vietnam War. The Foreign Minister's response made it clear that she had no wish to become involved in any way with what was happening in Vietnam.

On other occasions, along with Australian diplomats in many countries, I had to seek Israeli support for Australian candidacies in various international bodies. Although officials always received these representations sympathetically, Israel had no particular reason to support us and I do not recall ever receiving a formal reply or hearing that Israel had supported us.

In one instance, we did effect a change in Israeli policy. An Australian citizen, a Jew, born in Israel, had brought to our attention a seeming anomaly in the law that related to the obligations of Jews born in Israel to do Israeli military service. I forget the details of this, but we brought it to the attention of the Foreign Ministry who, rather to my surprise, agreed with us, and the Parliament (the Knesset) altered the law to correct the anomaly. Effecting a change to an Israeli law was something I do not think many other embassies in Tel Aviv succeeded in doing.

We had one or two matters of substance to take up with the Israelis, most of them concerned with property in Israel that had been confiscated from Arabs who had become Australian citizens after the War of Independence. The Israelis were not very forthcoming on these questions, even though a senior Foreign Ministry official once claimed that Mr Hood had "threatened" him about one of them. But, on the whole, we had no serious problems. These were to come later, after the war in 1967, and occupation of the Arab lands which led to accusations against Israel at the United Nations.

Looking back to those halcyon days of 1963-65, I can see that there were some clouds on the horizon. I once arranged for Ambassador Hood and myself to have a briefing from Israeli intelligence. We were told that there were three developments which the Israelis would not tolerate and over which they would have no hesitation in going to war. The first was interference with the National Water Carrier being constructed to bring water south from the Sea of Galilee (over Arab objections); the second was establishment of a Nasserite regime in Jordan; and the third was interference with the passage of Israeli ships through the Straits of Tiran to Aqaba. The latter was the development that led to the War of 1967 when Egypt closed the Strait.

Other worrying developments for the Israelis at that time were creation of the Palestine Liberation Organization (PLO) in 1964 and, at about the same time, of el Fatah, a terrorist group led by Yasser Arafat. The PLO, it cannot be too often said, was devoted to the destruction of the State of Israel and recovery of all the territory therein by the Arabs. After the PLO's early leadership had proved ineffective, Arafat was elected Chairman in February 1969 and the PLO, influenced in large part by el Fatah, embarked on a more militant course.

At the time, it was difficult to see how the PLO's goal could possibly be realised in view of the determination and strength of Israel. It seemed that the Arabs were set on a course that would eventually lead to some great disaster – for them, not the Israelis.

Another difficulty for Israel was changing Western attitudes. In the 1940s and 1950s, most liberal opinion in the West tended to support Israel against the Arabs. Israel was a democracy; it had "made the desert bloom"; it had progressive social policies; the Jews deserved a home of their own. The Palestinian Arabs were seen by many Westerners not to have looked after their own country and in some respects to have forfeited their right to it. Nor had they made the most of the opportunities they had been given by the United Nations and others to arrive at a compromise with the Jews about territory in Palestine. They had opposed everything and then lost the war for which they had been largely responsible.

By the time of my arrival, there were many diplomats in Israel who, while not anti-Israel, at least viewed it with suspicion. Israel was thought to be attempting to manufacture an atomic bomb which could have disastrous consequences for the balance of power in the region. One embassy in Tel Aviv maintained a scientific attaché whose major role was to ascertain if Israel was, indeed, making a bomb. Israeli secret service agents were believed to have been active in Europe and elsewhere eliminating the perceived enemies of Israel. In 1954, a special mission had been sent to Cairo to destroy an American Government instrumentality there and throw the blame on the Egyptians. The mission (uncharacteristically) failed and the Israeli Government had been acutely embarrassed. The Israeli authorities were perceived to be keeping the Arab population of Israel (about 15 per cent of the population) under careful control so that it did not develop into a political force. The Foreign Ministry irritated embassies by such things as attempting to trick them into compromising their governments' stands on the status of Jerusalem. Many diplomats believed they were being spied on. The officers of foreign armed services who served on the various United Nations military missions (and who were much more anti-Israeli than any embassy official) all had stories about Israeli trickery and bad faith. Others, such as archaeologists and journalists working in the Middle East were, almost without exception, very anti-Israeli.

I was influenced by these sentiments and began to feel more sympathy towards the Arabs. There seemed to be a real lack of concern in Israel about what had happened to the Arabs and a failure to understand that some magnanimous gesture by Israel was necessary if genuine peace were ever to be established. Such a gesture was eventually made on the White House lawn by Prime Minister Yitzhak Rabin in 1993, but it was a long time coming, as it was with Arafat.

I came to believe that Australia had no reason to get mixed up in the politics of the Middle East and that Australians, by and large, did not understand how politics were played in that part of the world or how high the stakes were. Nor, as I have already suggested, and as I realised even more clearly when I served in Jordan twenty years later, was there much point in expecting Middle East leaders to get very interested in what was happening in our part of the world. Their priorities lay in areas far removed from ours.

I mention these attitudes that foreigners had towards Israel in those days because it seems that such feelings increased after the Six Day War in 1967, a war which now seems to have done nobody any good. After the oil crisis of the early 1970s, the Western Europeans became more conscious of their oil requirements and also more sensitive to Arab terrorism. Relations between Western countries and Israel accordingly grew cooler.

Recent developments are outside the scope of this book, but they do not give much hope that the Israelis and Arabs will ever be truly reconciled. The fratricidal fighting amongst the Arabs has diverted attention from the Palestine problem, but it is still there and unlikely to go away.

Tel Aviv was a stimulating post. The Israel Philharmonic Orchestra was of world standard and many famous musicians played with it. Government ministers and officials were well informed and always willing to talk. Archaeological sites were well preserved and easy to visit. The Israelis were hospitable and easy to entertain. It was a remarkable posting

4
KENYA, 1965-68
Post-Colonial Afterglow

Before leaving Tel Aviv, I was informed that I was to be posted to Nairobi in Kenya to open the Australian High Commission there. Until that time, Australia had a trade commission. I first travelled to The Hague to meet the Ambassador there, Mr (subsequently Sir) Walter Crocker, who was likewise to be transferred to Kenya as the High Commissioner, to discuss arrangements for the new post. I was pleased when, without my mentioning it, he recalled that he knew my parents in New York in the 1940s. He kindly put his car at my disposal for an afternoon so I could see the Rembrandts and the Vermeers in The Hague. I then travelled to Nairobi, spending a few days in Rome, which I had never visited. I arrived in Nairobi on 5 September 1965; Crocker arrived several weeks later.

A cross-posting from one post to another can be difficult. One leaves a society that one has become accustomed to and moves to another society of which one has little knowledge. This can be a jolting experience. A posting from Canberra to a new environment can be an adventure and a return to Canberra is a return home. But one does not feel at home when moving to a new environment where nobody knows anything about the country from which one has just arrived. I certainly felt this when I arrived in Nairobi from Tel Aviv, especially as our relations with Kenya were so thin.

Many African states became independent in the 1950s and the 1960s, particularly after the British Prime Minister Harold Macmillan's famous "Winds of Change" speech in 1960. Until the 1950s, our only diplomatic posts in Africa had been in Egypt and South Africa. Australia opened a High Commission in Ghana after it became independent: we opened later in Nigeria and Tanganyika (now Tanzania). The Government wanted to establish presences in Africa to monitor developments and to influence the policies of host governments. At that time, also, southern African affairs, notably in South Africa and Rhodesia (now Zimbabwe), were attracting world-wide interest which demanded our attention. These questions were of great interest to the Commonwealth of Nations and, at that time, the Commonwealth Heads of Government meetings were among the most important events attended by a Prime Minister of Australia.

The High Commissioner was to be resident in Nairobi, but also to be accredited to the neighbouring states of Ethiopia and Uganda. The proposal to establish diplomatic relations with these three countries was first put to their embassies in Washington by our Embassy there. The replies from Uganda and Ethiopia were relatively quick, but the Kenyans took much longer to respond, almost to the point of causing our Government some inconvenience in the timing of its plans to post officers to Nairobi. This led to speculations that the Kenyan Government had difficulties with our immigration policies (although the White Australia policy was on its last legs at that time).

It was possibly more administrative confusion than anything else that caused the delay. The Chief of Protocol in Nairobi welcomed Mr Crocker and myself with the utmost cordiality and politeness on arrival. Later we heard he had been involved in a colossal corruption scandal; he probably had other things on his mind than White Australia when he welcomed us. Certainly, the Kenyan Government never tackled us about Australia's racial policies, apart from the fact that senior officials in the foreign ministry would sometimes tease us about them. The only "racial" problem we ever had was when the Australian pop group, The Seekers, was banned from performing in Nairobi because it had performed before racially segregated audiences in South Africa. But the Australian Government had no involvement in that.

In those days, the Department of External Affairs seemed to think that being sent to open a new post was akin to a rite of passage or a coming of age. Certainly, opening the post was the most important thing I did in Nairobi. We had to find an office, buy a residence for the High Commissioner, find rented accommodation for other officers and furnish all these properties. We also had to find staff. It proved unusually difficult to find either an office or residential accommodation. Many people had left Kenya on independence, but other people had moved in – embassies, business, banks, etc., all with demands for property. One problem was that the rent ceilings set by the regulatory authorities in Canberra were much lower than the prevailing rents in Nairobi.

We took so long to find residential accommodation that our overlords in Canberra thought we were dragging our feet. Then, suddenly, almost by accident, an Italian businessman in the up-market area of Nairobi decided to sell his house and we managed to persuade Canberra to buy it. It is still the High Commissioner's residence. We also found some rooms in the Indian Life Insurance Building and these suited our purpose at the time, although we vacated them and moved into a newer building not long after I left Kenya. We were fortunate enough to find an interior decorator, the wife of the former Chief Justice of the Sudan, who managed to furnish the residence and the office to our requirements. All this took at least six months and prevented us from getting down to our work.

Kenya became independent from the United Kingdom on 12 December 1963. The following year it became a Republic with Jomo Kenyatta as President. The population in 1965 was nine and half million.

Australia did not have any great interest in internal affairs of the three countries. Kenya was of particular interest because the transition to independence after the Mau Mau terrorist period in the 1950s to the presidency of Jomo Kenyatta had been achieved smoothly, mainly through the efforts of Kenyatta himself and Malcolm MacDonald, the British Governor and subsequently High Commissioner. MacDonald had been able to persuade the British Government that Kenyatta was not a "leader to darkness and death" as had been prophesied by a previous Governor but an enlightened and tolerant ruler, as proved to be the case. As the son of the first Labour Prime Minister of the United Kingdom, Ramsay MacDonald, Malcolm MacDonald, himself a former Cabinet minister, had great influence in London. Kenyatta persuaded the British settlers who had been farming in Kenya to remain, thus maintaining the economy. He appointed a European, Bruce Mackenzie, as the Minister for Agriculture. The Speaker of Parliament, Humphrey Slade, was also European. If any major lesson became clear during my time in Nairobi, it was that a smooth transition to an independent, multi-racial state could take place and could be maintained.

MacDonald (1901-81) had been a Cabinet minister for most of the 1930s and was responsible for the White Paper of 1939 which proposed an end to further Jewish migration to Palestine, thus incurring the wrath of the Zionists. Subsequently, he became High Commissioner to Canada, Governor-General of Malaya, Commissioner-General for South-East Asia, and High Commissioner to India.

Kenyatta, although by now an old man, did prove an inspiring and magnanimous leader, much better than his successor, Moi. He had been involved allegedly in the Mau Mau movement of the 1950s but by the mid-1960s there was surprisingly little talk about Mau Mau. Most of the old-time settlers used to joke about the absurd antics their own people had performed during the emergency.

Another politician of standing was Tom Mboya, a Cabinet minister who might have turned out to be a worthy successor to

Malcolm MacDonald (white suit), American Chargé Wendell Coote, Richard Gate, President of Malawi, Dr Hastings Banda, and President Kenyatta of Kenya, Nairobi, 1967

Kenyatta had he not been assassinated. He was, however, from the Luo, the rival tribe to the dominant Kikuyu which was Kenyatta's tribe. Mboya might not have been able to attract the loyalty of the Kikuyu. The Luo was the tribe from which United States President Barack Obama's father emerged. Another interesting personality was the suave and sophisticated Attorney-General, Charles Njonjo, usually referred to as a "black Englishman". Whatever ambitions he might have had evaporated when he fell completely from favour sometime after I left Kenya. Mboya did actually visit Australia at our invitation, so great was his reputation.

There was some concern about the possible penetration into Africa, and Kenya in particular, by Chinese communism. Oginga Odinga, the nation's first Vice-President, favoured closer relations with China whereas Kenyatta looked to the West. Odinga was reputed to have once said "communism is food", a remark which led him to be regarded with some suspicion. By the time we arrived in Kenya, however, the Chinese diplomats had been expelled from Kenya and it seems doubtful if Chinese influence was ever very great.

We almost never had to make representations to the Kenyan Government on matters of substance. The only time I recall having done so was to seek its support for an Australian candidate to be a member of the International Court of Justice. The official laughed in my face at my effrontery as the incumbent Australian judge (Sir Percy Spender) on the Court had just voted against a case which the African states had brought before it.

One unexpected intimacy in Australian-Kenyan relations occurred after the death of Harold Holt. The High Commission was visited by two African ministers who wanted to convey their condolences. During their visit it became clear that they were completely mystified by the fact that a Prime Minister could have disappeared on a beach while he was swimming and completely unattended by security guards.

Ethiopia was of interest to Australia partly because it was the seat of the Organization for African Unity (OAU) which was considered likely to have great influence on the development of African affairs. The OAU has probably turned out to be less influential than we expected.

Ethiopia also enjoyed high prestige because, like Liberia, it had retained its independence when most of the rest of Africa had been colonised. The Emperor, Haile Selassie, was a recognised leader and concerns were being expressed about what would happen to Ethiopia when he disappeared, as he did early in the 1970s. It was also the site of an important American defence base when the Cold War expanded into Africa.

The Emperor ran a highly personalised form of government, with spies and informers everywhere. I once had a vivid example of this. I was walking along the street when the Emperor passed by in his car. A woman rushed out and threw something at the car. Thinking I was about to witness the assassination of a world figure, I looked on with apprehension. The car stopped, a man got out, picked up whatever the woman had thrown at the car and gave it to the Emperor. It then became clear that the woman had thrown a petition to Haile Selassie who then proceeded to read it carefully. Evidently, this was the way his subjects brought to his attention matters that concerned them and he took notice of them immediately.

Australia was not unknown in Ethiopia. Dr Reginald Hamlin (now deceased) and his wife, Dr Catherine Hamlin, had been in Ethiopia since 1959 where they founded the Addis Ababa Fistula Hospital which was the only medical centre in the world dedicated exclusively to providing free obstetric fistula repair surgery to poor women suffering from child-birth injury. They were highly regarded by the Ethiopian Government and people. Catherine Hamlin has also received many Australian awards and is a Companion of the Order of Australia. A Sydney ferry has also been named after her. Certainly the Hamlins were the best known Australians who had ever been associated with Ethiopia.

The Hamlins' prestige may have been the reason we were accorded special treatment when we asked for accreditation from Nairobi. Until then, Ethiopia had never accepted dual accreditation where the ambassador was resident in a country to its south. This was undoubtedly because the Emperor considered countries to the south of Ethiopia to be less important than those to its north.

The Emperor did, indeed, visit Australia several months after I left East Africa in 1968. He had a pet dog which travelled with him wherever he went in his plane. We had to explain firmly to the Ethiopian officials that, if the dog came to Australia, it would be destroyed instantly on arrival because of our quarantine regulations. I never learned what happened as a result of this warning. I believe there was a similar incident some time ago when an African president arrived in Australia with a plane-load of frogs which it was his habit to consume.

Relations between Uganda and Australia were thin. The then Prime Minster, Apollo Milton Obote, was not firmly in the saddle. The curious composition of the state, a federation of five Kingdoms with the king of the biggest, the Kabaka of Buganda, as the head of state, was unlikely to last long. Obote did not last long and was overthrown in 1971 by the notorious Idi Amin. Obote did, however, make a brief comeback after Amin's fall. Uganda is the only country I ever visited where I made a mental note, after my arrival, that I never wanted to visit it again.

We had virtually no aid programs to these countries at that time, apart from some scholarships. Our aid efforts were directed mainly to Asia.

The High Commissioner, W. R. Crocker, had been recruited to the diplomatic service at head of mission level in 1952 by the then Minister for External Affairs, R. G. Casey. Born in Broken Hill in 1902, Crocker had been educated at the University of Adelaide, Balliol College, Oxford, and Stanford in the United States. He entered the British Colonial Service and served in Nigeria in the 1930s. After leaving the service, he worked for the International Labour Office in Europe and joined the British army during the war where he attained the rank of Colonel. After the war, he was head of the Africa Section at the United Nations Secretariat in New York. He then returned to Australia as Professor of International Relations at the newly-established

Australian National University in Canberra in 1949. Subsequently Casey appointed him High Commissioner to India in 1952. Casey admired him because he had "led a life of action". While doing all these other things, Crocker had published several books on subjects such as the Japanese population problem, self-government for the colonies and race relations in international affairs.

The Australian High Commissioner, Mr W. R. (later Sir Walter) Crocker, presenting credentials to President Jomo Kenyatta of Kenya, Nairobi, 1965

By the time he arrived in Nairobi, Crocker had served as head of mission in India (twice), Indonesia, Canada and The Hague. Most heads of mission who had served in such senior posts might have thought that Nairobi was a distinct come down, but Crocker, because of his previous service in Nigeria and the United Nations, had sympathy for Africans and an interest in them. After leaving the British service, he had written a book on Nigeria critical in some ways of British administration there. This had had a *succes d'estime et de scandale* which made him well-known in colonial circles. Even in 1965, when he arrived in Nairobi, there were a sufficient number of old-time British officials working either in the British High Commission or the Kenyan public service who remembered him. His arrival caused a frisson of excitement amongst them: "It can't be Crocker" was their response. While he was in Nairobi, he published (in England) a book on Nehru. This was dismissed by an Indian reviewer in Kenya with the remark that "this pompous book can do only harm". I thought it was a serious and thoughtful work, sympathetic but not uncritical. It dealt with Nehru's prime ministership, the Indian conflict with China and racial questions.

Partly because of his wide-ranging career, Crocker had a considerable interest in many spheres of life. He was probably not great in an academic sense, but if any subject came up for discussion such as colonial wars in the Gold Coast, the creation of Israel, African exploration, the political effects of the writings of Freud, criticisms of the music of Brahms, the emergence of women doctors in England, or Indian attitudes to colonialism, Crocker would always have a pertinent comment to make.

He had his prejudices, but here he was not consistent. He did not believe that Americans had the capacity to assume the world leadership that fell to them after the Second World War. Nevertheless, he had close relationships with many eminent Americans including Walter Lippmann. He was often critical of Jews, especially in matters affecting Israel, but he valued the judgment of many Jews such as Isaiah Berlin and worshipped Yehudi Menuhin. He had many sides to his character and it was always necessary to be on guard, wondering what his reaction would be to any remark or situation.

My parents had met him several times in New York when he was at the United Nations and, on the basis of this acquaintance, I asked him for a reference when I applied for entrance to a university college in Melbourne in 1952. He replied with a most flowery document which said, amongst other things, that I had sufficient talent to be a professional musician. This was manifestly untrue and led the college which admitted me to think it was receiving some kind of musical genius, an assumption which was of some embarrassment to me.

One of my colleagues, who had served with him in another post, told me that, at one stage, Crocker had become obsessed with the idea that he (Crocker) was about to die. From that moment, my colleague's working hours, and many of his non-working hours, were devoted to preparing for Crocker's death, which did not take place until well after the posting was over and Crocker was 100.

Crocker had the reputation in the service of being "difficult". There was some truth in this. If he did not like or value a particular officer in his embassy, he would refuse to acknowledge or speak to him. When he left Nairobi to go on leave to Australia, or at any other time, he would refuse to inform the Foreign Ministry or appoint an acting Head of Mission. This meant that, had any serious matter arisen between the mission and the Foreign Ministry, the Kenyan Government would have been entitled not to receive the views of the mission on the grounds that there was nobody to speak for it. He seemed to have a Louis XIV attitude towards the High Commission: he was the High Commission; if he were not there, there was no High Commission.

I myself did not find him impossible to deal with. After I had learned and understood his foibles and prejudices, I was able to work around them. I had no serious trouble with him and the High Commission worked well, in large part due to the help I received from other members of the staff. As already mentioned, before going to Nairobi, I flew from Tel Aviv to see Crocker in The Hague, at the Department's direction. He cabled that he was looking forward to seeing me so that we could discuss such important matters as the purchase of a radiogram for his residence. As we did not even have an office in Nairobi at that stage, let alone a residence, this caused me to have doubts about his capacity as an administrator; those doubts were later confirmed. The interview in The Hague went quite well, although he told me that if I wore awful clothes, came late to the office or told lies, I would be "sent home". I was happy to abide by these injunctions. On the whole, however, he took an interest in his staff and their problems. He was also, surprisingly, capable of sudden and impulsive kindnesses.

Crocker was an excellent writer and stylist and his reports were read widely in the government. Prime Minister Menzies once commented on one of his despatches about Nepal: "this is fascinating". When he left Jakarta, he wrote six despatches covering all aspects of Indonesian life and politics. These found their way into the embassies of other countries and attracted a degree of fame. Even as late as the early 2010s, recruits to the Department of Foreign Affairs and Trade were being directed to these despatches as models of reporting. In his books, his writing was often restrained but in his departmental reports he pulled no punches. Once, the head of the Department ordered that several sentences in one of his despatches be excised with a pair of scissors as they were thought to reflect unfairly on another senior member of the public service. Sometimes there was some doubt as to whether his remarks were based on fact or his imagination. When he reported that, before the granting of landing rights to an American airline in Kenya, a large sum of money changed hands, one wondered how he knew. On the whole, however, his reports reflected his wide experience and his interest in many aspects of international and national affairs and history.

In one particular respect, his previous record was of importance to Australia in Nairobi. He and Malcom MacDonald had been High Commissioners together in India. MacDonald had been Governor of Kenya before independence in 1963 and became High Commissioner after independence. By the time we were in Kenya, he was British Special Representative for Southern Africa and often travelled to the then Rhodesia where the Unilateral Declaration of Independence had just been promulgated by the

Prime Minister, Ian Smith. MacDonald was able and willing to brief Crocker fully on these developments.

Life in Nairobi at this time was not unlike that in a big Australian country town. The town itself reflected the rural activities that had been introduced by the European settlers. There was the one legitimate theatre which produced such shows as *The Merry Widow*. There were two newspapers, supermarkets, hotels, banks, stockbrokers, a small concert hall and a university. There were dog shows and horse shows and flower shows. The Muthaiga and Nairobi Clubs provided facilities for any kind of sport and also for swimming. Europeans lived in comfortable houses surrounded by spacious gardens in attractive suburbs. Although there was no legal apartheid, the considerable Indian population lived in Indian communities separate from the European areas. Those Africans who were at the bottom of the economic scale lived mostly outside the city in what were, in effect, slums.

The security situation was not perfect although none of us ever had any serious trouble. Kenya is often a cold country and the African population often lacked sufficient warm clothing. Europeans were seen as easy and legitimate targets for clothes. Most Europeans maintained night watchmen, burned outside lights all night and kept watchdogs. Africans had developed clever ways of stealing clothes, such as by poking fishing poles through house windows and picking up any spare clothes with fish hooks.

The lifestyles of the descendants of the English aristocracy who had settled in Kenya years before were a source of interest. The Happy Valley crowd, with their adulteries, drinking, drug-taking, murders and other accomplishments, had largely disappeared. The murder of the Earl of Erroll in 1941 was still discussed. The Earl had been found shot in his Buick. Everybody had his or her own idea about the guilty party. Lady Delamare, who had been the wife of the main (acquitted) suspect at the time, was still in Kenya and remained remarkably beautiful, but the only time I ever saw her was when she and I entered our dogs in a competition (mine won third prize). Some of those who did remain were single women whose husbands or parents had died and who nevertheless remained on their country properties alone, surrounded by African workers.

I came to know one of these well. Miss Pamela Montagu-Douglas-Scott was the grand-daughter of one of the Dukes of Buccleuch and the cousin of the then Duke. She was the first cousin of Princess Alice, the Duchess of Gloucester, who had lived in Australia when her husband was Governor-General. She came therefore from the highest rank of the British aristocracy but was remarkably relaxed about it. On her mother's side, she was descended from the Earls of Minto, two of whom, including her grandfather, had been Viceroys of India. She had an old engraving on the wall of an earlier Earl with his hand clutching a map of Java; he had seized Java for the Crown during his Viceroyalty. Pam's parents had built a huge stone house, "Deloraine", obviously based on a Scottish mansion, near Lake Nakuru in upcountry Kenya. The fireplace in the living room was so big that two people could have sat in it comfortably while the fire was burning. She reared cattle on 20,000 acres. The farm seemed quite successful and she ran it according to her own principles, using animals and workers. She hated farm machinery because she said it could not be eaten, it did not reproduce and it did not produce manure.

I was surprised when I first visited Deloraine to find that I was expected to come to dinner in pyjamas and dressing gown (preferably a very fancy one, which I did not have). This habit dated from the earlier days when a day's hard work in the fields was followed by a deep bath and grand dinner for which night attire was considered entirely suitable. On entry, one signed a visitors' book and was impressed to notice some of the other signatories, also dating from earlier times – Edward, P., Albert, P., Henry, P., and so on. Princess Alice had spent some time at

Miss Pamela Montagu-Douglas-Scott in her garden at Deloraine in Kenya

Deloraine before her marriage and the house was decorated with her many beautiful watercolours of the district.

The bedrooms were not what I was accustomed to in Australia. A magnifying glass was provided in case it was required to scrutinise something closely. Sealing wax was also provided in case it was necessary to send a sealed billet-doux, via a servant, to the person in the next room. These were relics of very bygone times which Pam had not bothered to eliminate. She often told amusing stories of the somewhat eccentric habits of her parents and their contemporaries. A more alarming menace was that, when the lights all went off at about 11.00 p.m., it became obvious that bats were flying in and out of the bedroom, occasionally grazing one's face with their wings.

The habits of a small creature known as the hyrax clashed with the aristocratic ambience of Deloraine. It is a rodent-looking animal which is said to be the closest relative to the elephant which it does not in any way resemble. It is omnivorous and apparently fearless. Often, when we were enjoying tea on the veranda or a meal in the dining room, a hyrax would take a flying leap from somewhere in the garden, land on the table and devour as much food as possible before being shooed away. Even more alarming was its propensity to get under the bed at night and issue a long piercing shriek just as one was drifting off to sleep. There seemed to be no way to avoid this disturbance.

There were other single women in much the same situation as Pam Scott. Ann Joyce reared cattle in 5000 acres on the Athi Plains, just south of Nairobi. Billie Dew did the same on a farm in the Rift Valley. These women lived alone surrounded by African servants and workers. It is a tribute both to them and their African employees that they were able to live for years safely in districts where public security was not always maintained.

Coming from Israel, where there was a wealth of historical sights and archaeological activities, I was rather disappointed at the lack of such things in Kenya. There were, however, some items of interest on the Kenya coast, including the very impressive Fort Jesus constructed by the Portuguese in Mombasa.

Ethiopia was, however, a very different matter and I was able to visit it a number times. The castles at Gondar, dating from the 17th century and combining Portuguese and Indian styles, were grand and fascinating. The magnificent rock-hewn churches in Lalibela date from the 11th or 12th centuries and are testimony to Ethiopia's long tradition of Christianity. The grandiose obelisks and other remains in Axum are believed to be more than 1700 years old and have become symbols of the Ethiopians' identity.

An unexpected pleasure was the charming city of Asmara, the capital of Eritrea, now an independent state. It was the capital of the Italian colony of Eritrea and the city itself is, or at least was when I saw it in the 1960s, an Italian town transported to Africa. In those days, the British and the Americans maintained consulates there and these were considered some of the most desirable "sleepers" in their foreign services – postings which were unexpectedly enjoyable.

Paul Hasluck was Minister for External Affairs most of the time I was in Nairobi and also for part of the time I was in Tel Aviv (as already related). Hasluck always insisted that anything submitted to him, or anything that left his office, be absolutely accurate in fact and in style. It was surprising then that the only two documents I received from him each contained an egregious error.

The letter to Mrs Golda Meir, to which I have already referred, was addressed to "Mrs Golda Meir, Minister for Foreign Affairs, Tel Aviv". The Israelis have for many years insisted that their capital city is Jerusalem and are very sensitive on this point. Australia and many other nations have never accepted this because they insist that the status of Jerusalem must be determined when the final settlement is made, if ever, between Arabs and Jews and have maintained their embassies in Tel Aviv. As soon as I noticed that Mrs Meir had been addressed as being in Tel Aviv, I knew that she would notice it also and would assume that we were making a political point. She could well have refused to receive the letter. I therefore explained, as soon as I met her, that the letter had been incorrectly addressed inadvertently and that I knew the Minister was not trying to revive the question of the status of Jerusalem. She accepted this, but it was touch and go.

The second error occurred when I was in Nairobi. Canberra had instructed us to conclude a war graves agreement with Ethiopia and we were sent a text of the agreement which we were to ask the Ethiopians to sign. Crocker and I travelled to Addis Ababa for this purpose but, when we arrived, I noticed that the agreement referred throughout to "the Kingdom of Ethiopia". Ethiopia was, however, an Empire and its ruler was an Emperor. Any suggestion that it was a mere Kingdom would have been completely unacceptable. We therefore had to return to Nairobi with the agreement unsigned and ask for a new text.

As is perhaps obvious from the above, Nairobi was not a very relevant post politically. Nor did it touch on Australia's vital interests. It was comfortable and sociologically interesting. Our task was a pioneering one of opening a presence in that part of Africa. Since my time there, the post has assumed accreditation to some other countries in East Africa.

For about six weeks in 1967 I was sent to Cairo from Nairobi to be charge d'áffaires as the Ambassador had to leave the post because of ill-health. Unfortunately, almost as soon as I arrived I fell ill myself of some Egyptian disease and was out of action for more than a week. Nevertheless, Cairo was a fascinating experience. This was just after the Six Day War between Israel and the Arab States and the city was empty of tourists which meant it was easy to move around. Every afternoon after work I would go out and look at some of the splendid mosques and other Islamic monuments in Cairo. It was also fascinating to fly from Nairobi to Cairo and follow the Nile as it flowed northwards with extensive greenery hugging the river on either side. Social contact with Egyptians was not easy, however, as the government was suspicious of foreigners after the disaster of the Six Day War.

5

NAURU, 1970-72

A Pacific Paradise?

After Nairobi, I was seconded to the Department of Labour and National Service in Melbourne for two years in accordance with an exchange scheme which existed between the two departments. That experience is worth a book in itself. At least, it did give me some experience at working in another government department away from Canberra.

Upon its conclusion, I was appointed the Australian Government Representative in Nauru. I arrived there on 5 September 1970, exactly five years after I had arrived in Nairobi.

Nauru became independent on 1 January 1968. Prior to that, it had been the subject of a League of Nations Mandate and a United Nations Trusteeship. In each case, the Mandate and the Trusteeship had been awarded to Australia, New Zealand and the United Kingdom, with Australia as the administering power. The interest of these countries was extraction of phosphate which was undertaken by the British Phosphate Commissioners (the BPC) whose headquarters were in Melbourne. On independence, the Nauru Phosphate Corporation (the NPC) assumed the task of extracting and selling the phosphate. Nauru was admitted to the Commonwealth as a "Special" member, which meant it did not attend Commonwealth Heads of Government Meetings. I believe this was insisted upon by the British Prime Minister. It became a full member in 2000, having become a member of the United Nations the previous year. As I recall, the population when I arrived in 1970 was about four thousand; of which half were Nauruan and the other half Gilbert and Ellice Islanders (from the countries now called Kiribati and Tuvalu) who worked the phosphate mines. There was a sprinkling of Chinese mechanics and electricians who worked for the phosphate corporation and probably about 300 Europeans who worked for the phosphate corporation and the government.

The Japanese occupied Nauru during the Second World War and transferred 1,200 Nauruans as labourers to the island of Truk (now Chuuk), one of the Federated States of Micronesia. The Nauruans endured great hardships during this period until they were repatriated after the war. It is interesting to recall that a Swiss Catholic priest, a Father Cleavaz, who had been in Nauru for some years, also went to Truk for the period of the Nauruans' captivity and was still in Nauru when I arrived in 1970.

The Australian Government sent a diplomat with the title of Australian Representative to Nauru shortly after independence. The first Representative was Mr J. C. B. Jackson, a surveyor who had worked in Nauru previously for the then Department of Territories. I was the first representative to come from the Department of External Affairs.

There had been some difficulties with the Nauruans. Australia had refused to appoint a High Commissioner because the Nauruans were not able to appoint a Nauruan as High Commissioner to Australia resident in Canberra. In the absence of an Australian High Commissioner, the President of Nauru had concluded that the Australian Representative was a not a very influential figure in Australian diplomacy and he did not regard him as an important channel of communication between himself and the Australian Government. My successor, Mr L. G. Sellars, did arrive on the island with the title of High Commissioner. By then, the Australian Government had changed its policy.

Life in Nauru was like being on a big ship for two years. The BPC had arranged a very comfortable lifestyle for its Australian staff in Nauru. The housing, although not luxurious, was adequate and well serviced. Ships came regularly to the island bringing supplies. There was a large shop which catered for our needs. A liquor store sold only the finest French wines; nobody would be seen drinking Australian wines!

These facilities were taken over by the NPC after independence. The NPC itself was managed largely by Australians in the service of the Nauru Government, although the work of extracting the phosphate was still undertaken by Gilbert and Ellice Islanders. Establishment of Air Nauru after independence increased the air services to the island. Facilities for sport were adequate. Mail came quickly and regularly by air.

Nauru was no tropical paradise, however. A reef around the island made surfing impossible and swimmers had to wear tennis shoes to avoid treading on stone fish. Some hardy souls took to snorkelling off the reef, facing encounters with sharks, and one young man was permanently crippled after contracting the bends. One day some Nauruans asked me to go out in a motor boat with them. The next day they went out again without me. The boat was dashed to pieces on the reef and they were left bobbing about in the Pacific for hours. I certainly would not have survived such an ordeal.

The office consisted of myself and a secretary/typist. We also had a locally-engaged Nauruan driver, but when he was bored on the job he would simply leave early. My job was to report on political, economic and social developments in Nauru, to extend consular assistance to Australians on the island (as well as to British nationals, Gilbert and Ellice Islanders and New Zealanders). I also had to issue visas to Nauruans and others wishing to visit Australia. I was also expected to attend every session of the Nauruan Parliament, which I duly did, often the only person in the public gallery. At tea break, I would join the members.

The Australian Government had decided in those days that Australians working on Nauru did not have to pay Australian income tax. This was evidently an inducement to Australians to accept job offers in Nauru but it seemed odd that it should apply to me as the representative of the Australian Government. I sought and received confirmation from the taxation authorities in Canberra that I would not have to pay tax. This was a financial benefit to me although it meant that I did not receive any allowances as would have normally been the case in an overseas posting. In any case, as there was not much to buy in Nauru, I saved quite a lot of money.

Pacific affairs then had a high profile in Canberra. The South Pacific Commission was still working from Noumea. The Pacific Forum held its first meeting at that time, largely as a result of an Australian initiative. Fiji and other Pacific entities were about to become, or had become, independent. The French nuclear tests in the Pacific were still a matter of controversy as was the question of independence for New Caledonia. I was therefore pleased when I came to realise that my reports were being widely read with interest in the Department in Canberra. I even received fan mail about them from people in far distant posts. That helped to overcome the inevitable feeling of isolation that I felt in Nauru.

Social life in Nauru was more varied than might have been expected. The Nauruans themselves were used to Australia and Australians and, although they were rather reserved and reticent, were quick to accept invitations. They rarely entertained in their own homes. The phosphate industry was a large scale enterprise in Nauru which meant that there was a wide variety of people working in it – accountants, engineers, doctors and ships captains, for example. Virtually all these people were Australians, as were most of the senior officials in the government. The Managing Director of the NPC, Mr T. A. Adams, had been a respected and well-known figure in the Australian mining industry. The Chief Secretary in the Government was an Irishman with wide experience of working in developing countries. The Chief Justice had been in the British army and had served in Cyprus and elsewhere. Two

President and Mrs Hammer DeRoburt of Nauru

young Australian doctors working in the NPC hospital later had distinguished careers in Australian hospitals. The Manager of the Bank of New South Wales (now Westpac), a New Zealander, was a solitary figure, not connected with the government, but with a view of his own about developments on the island.

A drive around the island took twenty minutes. The important activities were centred on one side of the island – the airport, the Parliament, the government offices, the main shops. Those Nauruans who lived on the other side of the island – ten minutes away – were regarded as hillbillies and the remarks made by their representatives in Parliament were greeted with guffaws. There was even a semblance of an aristocracy. Buraro Detudamo, member of the Cabinet and son of a former Head Chief, was educated at Knox College in Sydney, and had a prince-like, public schoolboy bearing.

Political life was dominated by President Hammer DeRoburt (1922-1992), a heavily built man of rather bilious aspect. Educated at the Geelong Institute of Technology, DeRoburt was certainly a very intelligent man. He spoke and wrote flawless English and was a man of remarkable perspicacity and far outshone his Cabinet colleagues. He knew he needed Australians to work on the island, but he resented Nauru's colonial past and was always on his guard for perceived slights.

The President ran a very personal government. He insisted that all important matters be channelled through him; he sometimes wrote his own invitations, sent his own telex messages and signed cheques for official purchases. He did not keep his minsters or his senior officials informed about what he was doing. He rarely made speeches in Parliament and gave vague answers to parliamentary questions. There was no newspaper and no other forum for public debate except Parliament which met infrequently. In particular, there was no public accounting of what was being done about the island's finances and many Nauruans believed that the President was spending far too much money on foreign travel and prestige projects that had little value. In his personal relations, however, the President was thoughtful and generous and it may have been this, as well as the fact that the Nauruans knew that he had no equal on the island, that led them to tolerate him for so long. He might have been more accountable had there been an organised opposition.

The President spent a great deal of time off the island, using the Air Nauru plane to travel all over the world, not only to Australia but also elsewhere. No information was ever given to the public as to where the President was or what he was doing. When he came home, he gave no public account of his travels. Partly this was due to the Pacific islands tradition of secrecy. In small societies, the only way in which anyone can retain any privacy is to maintain a strict silence about everything and to keep personal matters to oneself. I often had difficulty getting Nauruans to predict the weather.

In some Pacific islands, there had been some difficulty in reconciling the new Westminster system of government with the traditional island system. The Nauruan Local Government Council was established under the Trusteeship as a means of giving Nauruans some say in how they were governed. The

NLGC remained in existence after independence and it consisted of President DeRoburt and his four Cabinet ministers, an arrangement which prevented any conflict between the NLGC and the Government. One of the ministers explained to me that Nauruans found Parliament a rather oppressive institution as it had to take account of foreign reactions to and ambitions in Nauru, but in the NLGC only Nauruan interests were taken into consideration. I understood that the NLGC took many decisions on financial and other matters which the Government would have found embarrassing to disclose to Parliament.

Before I went to Nauru, I spoke with Sir William Dunk, a former very senior public servant in Canberra and later one of the British Phosphate Commissioners. He told me that DeRoburt would treat me very well "until something happened". Unfortunately, "something happened" not long after I arrived. DeRoburt decided he wanted to sack and deport the head of one of the government departments who had somehow displeased him. This man was an Australian and I immediately received representations from other Australians on the island to do something about it.

I therefore called on the President and said if he did deport the man, the Australian Government might object. I probably should not have done this as any government is free to deport whomever it likes. I could see that the President resented what I did and his attitude to me was never the same again. He refused to attend Australia Day celebrations, for example. Nevertheless, I continued to see the President on a regular basis in his office when he would give me a fairly good briefing on what was happening on the island and what his intentions were. No mention, however, was ever made about the island's finances.

The Government was, however, ignorant of diplomatic niceties and I often ran into problems. The President once made a speech in Parliament which, as I recall, suggested that Nauru might become a tax haven. Knowing that this would be of interest in

Canberra, I asked him for a copy of the speech, a request which would have been quite normal in almost any other country. The President refused at first, saying that the speech would not be available until Hansard was printed. As Hansard had never been printed and there was no prospect that it would ever be printed, there seemed little chance of getting the speech and I could see the President regarded my request as unwarranted prying.

On another occasion, a government official asked if I had anything to put in the Government Gazette. I had just received a notice from Canberra for all Australian citizens in Nauru concerning taxation matters. I suggested she put that in the Gazette. She did so and this caused a furore in government circles, particularly the President, because I had not sought permission to insert the notice. I was virtually ostracised for several days. My own attitude was that the official (an Australian) had approached me and it had been her job to know whether the notice was appropriate material for the Gazette.

The gaol was near the government offices and one day, as I was getting into my car after calling on a minister, some Nauruans asked if I could give them a lift back home. I willingly agreed. Afterwards I discovered that they had been escaped prisoners and that I had abetted their escape. It did not seem difficult to escape from the gaol. One muscular prisoner simply tore down the door and walked out.

At one stage, it was intimated to me that the President would appreciate very much being given a knighthood. He was apparently resentful that Ratu Sir Kamisese Mara, the Prime Minister of Fiji, had been knighted. I said it was usual for the Queen to knight only persons in states of which she was the Head of State. My interlocutors replied that Douglas Fairbanks, the screen actor, had been knighted, although he was an American. I replied that I thought Douglas Fairbanks and the President were somewhat different. Authorities in Canberra pointed out that Nauru could introduce its own form of knighthood, should it wish to do so.

I understand that much later the Queen gave the President an Honorary Knighthood.

The phosphate deposits were due to be exhausted by about 1995 (I understand they lasted for some time longer). The Government's policy was therefore to invest the royalties in economic entities and activities that would bring regular income in future years. It therefore established the Nauruan Shipping Line and Air Nauru and bought real estate in Australia, such as Nauru House in the CBD in Melbourne, and elsewhere. Even in those early days, it seemed doubtful if these efforts would succeed. The President used the airline for his own official travel, thus disrupting its schedules and causing customers to doubt the airline's reliability. The shipping line was plagued with problems. Its schedules were unreliable and other islands found they could not rely on it. Some of the ships were substandard and should not have been bought. It also seemed that the Government chose its Australian economic advisors not on the grounds of their expertise but because the Nauruans knew them and felt they could work with them. From the little I know of developments in Nauru since that time, it seems that our doubts in those days about the viability of these various enterprises were justified.

While in Nauru, I also had "visiting and reporting responsibilities" for the United States Trust Territory of the Pacific Islands and the British colony of the Gilbert and Ellice Islands. I paid a three-week visit to the TTPI and a shorter visit to the GEIC. In both cases, most of the discussions I had concerned the progress of those areas to self-government or independence.

While in the GEIC, I was the guest of the Governor, Sir John Field, and Lady Field, in Tarawa. Life in their residence was formal. At dinner, the men wore "Red Sea Rig", which consisted of black tie without a coat. After dinner, port was passed around the table clockwise with special care being taken not to let the bottle touch the table (this might result in a sailor being lost at sea).

Both territories faced much the same problems: shortage of land, lack of capital, shortage of trained labour, feeble infrastructure, long distances between islands, poor prospects for foreign investment and separatism within the islands themselves. On the whole the Americans seemed to have done a better job of educating a small elite. The American "get up and go" attitude was very noticeable; the British had not introduced this spirit into their colonies in the Pacific. There were some politicians in the TTPI of ability and ambition, although it was true that many of the educated classes were simply working in air-conditioned government offices and not contributing much to economic development of the territory. There was certainly much more public discussion of political and other matters in the TTPI than there was in Nauru or some of the other Pacific islands. On the whole, however, I left both areas with the impression that their futures were not promising. Fishing should have been a prospect, but shortage of live bait, lack of fishing fleets and absence of canning facilities seemed to be insurmountable problems.

One episode in the GEIC struck me as particularly sad. On the boat on which we were travelling was a young British man serving with Voluntary Service Overseas who was to land on one of the outer islands to "build a rest house". He spoke no Gilbertese, there was no one to meet him, he had nowhere to live, he had no supplies. The boat simply dumped him on the beach with a case of beer and left him to his fate. No other ship was expected at the island for three months.

Before I went to Nauru, a senior officer in External Affairs warned me not to stay a day longer than two years. I did stay one day longer, but without any visibly bad effects. On the whole, I enjoyed life there. There were no real discomforts, tennis was possible, food and drink were abundant and social life was sufficiently variable to be tolerable. The main disadvantage was the island's isolation; the nearest islands, the Gilbert and Ellice, were more than one hundred miles away.

6
ITALY, 1974-77
Will Italy go Communist?

After leaving Nauru, I spent two years in Canberra, mainly working in African affairs. I was then posted to Rome as Counsellor and arrived early in 1974. As soon as I arrived in Italy, I was sent to Florence for three months to learn Italian. I never became fluent, but at least I learned to read the newspapers, move around and handle my own personal affairs. It was in Florence, however, that I developed a great interest in Italian painting. My attention was first attracted to a Nativity by Ghirlandaio in the Church of St Trinita, just opposite the British Institute where I was learning Italian. It looked so fresh and glistening that it might have been painted the previous week.

From then on, every weekend while I was in Florence, I would take a bus and go to a neighbouring city – Siena, San Gimignano, Bologna, Arezzo – to see the paintings in galleries and churches. By the time I left Italy I must have seen every gallery in that country. I was very lucky later that my apartment in Rome was near to many of the Caravaggio paintings in Rome, most of them within walking distance.

Accommodation in Florence was difficult. At first I stayed in an apartment where the landlady rented rooms to people like myself. Here, the water pressure was most inadequate and I could not get any water at all to bathe in until midnight, and then only a trickle. I soon moved to a pensione on the Arno River. The bed was most uncomfortable because a door had been placed on top of the mattress to make the bed stiffer. I removed the door and was able to settle down to a reasonable life although, like all such places in Italy, the light globes were so weak it was difficult to read.

I soon learned that there were other problems in Italy. Toilets did not always flush properly; windows sometimes could not be opened or closed properly; buttons would never fit into button holes; dentists were hard to find; pickpockets abounded in the buses; footpaths were littered with dog manure; many shops and other useful entities closed in the afternoon just when one wanted them open. These things simply had to side-stepped in order to enjoy the attractions Rome had to offer.

One curious feature I noticed soon after I arrived was the presence in the trains of well-dressed, well-groomed middle aged men with smart briefcases who looked as if they were travelling to attend important meetings. No sooner had they sat down, however, than they would produce a Mickey Mouse comic book from their briefcases and read it with ferocious intensity, or pull out a drawing book in which they produced a picture by drawing lines from one numbered dot to the next. These activities seemed to occupy them for the entire journey.

The Campidoglio, Rome

ITALY, 1974-77

The Embassy consisted of a political section, a trade section, an immigration section, an administrative section and a small public affairs section. Some months before I arrived, it had been decided that the immigration section was vastly overstaffed and a considerable number of its members were dismissed. They took action against us in an Italian court and the judges, notwithstanding that, because we were an embassy we were immune from the Italian courts, decided the case against us and ordered us to take the employees back. We refused to do so, but the feelings against us among the former employees remained acute for some time.

Italy had had a tumultuous history after the Second World War. The old monarchy was abolished in a referendum in 1946. Italy's most important politician in the early post-war period was Alcide De Gasperi, founder of the Christian Democratic Party, a conservative party with close links to the Catholic Church. De Gasperi was Prime Minister from 1945 until 1953. Under his leadership, Italy retained a degree of political stability and took the first steps in the Italian "economic miracle". From about 1960, however, there were more or less constant changes of government, all of them dominated by the Christian Democrats who, however, in the early 1960s, made an "opening to the left" towards the Socialist Party.

Few of us heading for Rome in those days had any idea of the heady atmosphere we were about to experience. In the early 1970s, a catastrophe in Italy seemed likely. It was hit by the oil crisis, inflation, a balance of payments problem, serious disagreement amongst party leaders, ministerial resignations, difficult demands by union leaders, allegations of corruption, threats of coups and political violence. Riots over political and economic matters in the streets were frequent; some days it was even difficult to get to work. The climax to all this occurred sometime after I left Rome when a former Prime Minister, Aldo Moro, was kidnapped and then murdered by the Red Brigades.

The main political question in Italy at the time was the future of the Italian Communist Party (the PCI), then led by the late Enrico Berlinguer and the second most important political party in Italy. In 1973 the PCI had announced a new doctrine, the "Historic Compromise", in which it declared that it would be willing to work with "bourgeois" parties, perhaps in a coalition of some kind. This possibility caused some alarm amongst Western allies. In particular, Dr Henry Kissinger, then the Secretary of State in the Nixon Administration, declared that communists were unacceptable in NATO governments.

My impression was that Italians lacked confidence in their own government's ability to determine what was to happen in Italy. Many believed, for example, that the "opening to the left" that took place early in the 1960s had been the initiative of President Kennedy. Now, they were convinced that, if the communists entered the Government, the CIA would immediately mount a coup to bring it down. They believed that this is what had been Chile's fate several years earlier when President Allende had been removed and a military regime under General Pinochet had been installed. So important was this example to them that the Diplomatic List had not been re-issued for years because the Italians could not bring themselves to admit that the Pinochet Government in Chile, or its representatives in Rome, was legitimate. What was difficult for foreigners to understand was that the Italians felt completely helpless against the supposed machinations of the CIA.

There was no doubt that the Communist Party was popular. The most successful vote getter after the Christian Democrats, it had a huge mass-membership. Many film stars and film directors were followers of the party. The great pianist Maurizio Pollini embraced causes that were dear to the PCI. It was considered chic in many quarters to be a supporter of the party. Communist administrators in some cities were efficient and gave the people what they wanted. Bologna was the prime example. The management of opera houses was divided amongst the political parties. The communists had not, however, reached as far as the management of La Scala in Milan which was, if I recall correctly, in the hands of the Socialists. The communists held their rallies in the huge square of the church of San Giovanni in Laterano in Rome because only they could fill that vast area with their supporters. The party leader, Enrico Berlinguer, with his windswept hair, was something of a folk hero. When the party claimed it was the only party whose hands were clean, many believed them. There was a feeling that the Communist Party would eventually be given a place in government. What would happen afterwards worried people.

The party had gone some way to divorce itself from traditional Soviet-style policies, although I understand that post-Soviet intelligence has shown that the PCI was in receipt of Soviet funds during the 1970s. It had declared that it was opposed to nationalisation of the means of production and that it was not opposed to foreign investment. It had accepted Italy's membership of the European Community and NATO. It distanced itself from some of the Soviet Union's declared foreign policy aims. It had declared that it eschewed revolution and would aim to secure power through the ballot box; it would always accept the decision of the ballot box and would respect other parties. It had certainly played a useful role in Parliament in passing, or at least not blocking, useful legislation.

But not everybody trusted the communists. Many pointed out that their policies amounted to nothing more than slogans and desirable goals. They believed that the communists, if in power, would tolerate other parties only if those parties supported communist policies. They were suspicious of the party's ties with the Soviet Union. And they felt that the assumption of power by the communists would lead to civil strife and possible foreign interference.

Finally, there is always the possibility that Berlinguer did not have the stomach to assume power whether in coalition with other parties or not. He might have thought that the risk was too great and would have disastrous consequences. He might have been happier sitting on the sidelines, being seen as a responsible party leader and enjoying the undoubted reputation he had as the most respected man in Italian politics.

At the Embassy, we tried to follow all this as best we could. The Embassy possessed two first class officers who later became stars in the public service – Michael Thawley, later Ambassador to the United States and, later still, the Secretary of the Department of Prime Minister and Cabinet, and Paul O'Sullivan, later Ambassador to Germany, High Commissioner in New Zealand and the Director-General of ASIO. Both spoke Italian fluently and kept in touch with the Communist Party. I spoke frequently with the American Embassy.

All this came to a head with parliamentary elections in 1976. The communists won 38 per cent of the vote, as did the Christian Democrats. I left Italy not long afterwards, but I think that that represented the high point of the communists' popularity. Afterwards things started to go downhill for them. Berlinguer died in 1984.

The Embassy also had frequent contact with the Italian Foreign Ministry on a wide range of subjects ranging from the Middle East to energy. The Italians were always very forthcoming and seemed to have a gift for diplomacy not always noticeable in other foreign ministries. I was lucky enough to get to know the Prime Minister's advisor on foreign affairs, Umberto La Rocca, who kept me informed after he attended the G-6 and other important international meetings. Of particular interest were the Conferences on Security and Co-operation in Europe which seemed to offer at least a glimmer of hope that some chinks might be made in the Iron Curtain. There was no indication whatsoever that in a little more than a decade the Curtain would come down entirely.

As is often the case in large posts, we did not see a great deal of other diplomatic missions. The New Zealand Embassy was nearby, in an obscure part of town where there were no other missions, so neighbourliness kept us in touch. We also saw the Americans because they had a great interest in the future of the Communist Party and a good deal of economic expertise. The British Embassy was particularly useful on labour relations and the Commonwealth connection was also important. In the Italian government, our most important contacts, outside the Foreign Ministry, were with the economic ministries through which we tried to keep in touch with the disastrous Italian economy.

There were the usual round of cocktail parties and national day celebrations. One Italian woman, who bore a remarkable resemblance to Charles II, used to crash these parties so persistently that in the end the embassies simply invited her, although I do not think Australia did as we did not know her name.

For some years the Australian Department of Foreign Affairs had been subsidising the presence at the University of Venice of an Australian, the late Professor Bernard Hickey, a Queenslander. Hickey had achieved the seemingly impossible task of securing a permanent lectureship at the University and taught Australian literature. As far as we could judge, his courses were successful and he himself was well known in Venice, having been friends with Peggy Guggenheim and Ezra Pound. Shortly before I left Italy, the Department organised a seminar in Venice, under Hickey's leadership, of people, both Australian and otherwise, who taught Australian literature throughout Europe, ranging from Denmark to Yugoslavia. The seminar was also attended by a number of Australian literary figures including Thea Astley. Professor Hickey later left Venice and went on to conduct his courses at the University of Lecce.

There was a small theatre in the Embassy and sometimes

visiting Australian artists – a string quartet or a pianist – would present a concert. These were usually well attended by invitees. On one occasion, attendance was comparatively low because the weather had been very bad and the roads were slippery and wet. I sent a long memorandum to the Department explaining exactly what had happened. This was picked up by one of those committees of inquiry which the Whitlam Government was fond of creating to examine the public service. The committee declared that the memorandum was absurd and completely irrelevant to any work the Embassy should have been doing. I still stand by what I said.

Another cultural manifestation was an exhibition of paintings by ten Australian artists which the Department sent to Italy. It was curated by Ron Radford, then the director of the Ballarat Art Gallery. The exhibition was mounted in Rome, Florence, Venice and Milan. It attracted good crowds but the Italian art critics were rather dismissive. This was patronising as there was little of much value being painted by Italians in Italy at that time.

There were some Australian musicians in Italy who had carved out careers for themselves there. Maureen Jones was, and, I believe, still is, a well-known pianist internationally, as well as in Italy. The soprano Margaret Baker-Genovesi, now retired in Brisbane, sang successfully throughout the peninsula

But the most important Australian manifestation which occurred when I was in Italy was the visit in late 1974 and early 1975 of Prime Minister Whitlam, his wife and an enormous entourage. Before his arrival, a fog had descended on Rome's main airport (which had never happened before) making it impossible for planes to land. The welcoming party had to drive as fast as possible to another airport on the other side of town. Luckily we arrived before the plane landed. The Italians took the visit seriously, partly because there were so many Italian migrants in Australia. The entire party was put up in Rome's best hotel and showered with gifts.

ITALY, 1974-77

Prime Minister Aldo Moro of Italy greets Prime Minister Gough Whitlam, Rome, 1974

Mr Whitlam had discussions with the Prime Minister, Aldo Moro, and the President hosted a lunch for him. Senior officials were able to have serious discussions with their Italian counterparts. Then disaster struck in the shape of Cyclone Tracy in Darwin. Mr Whitlam had to fly home, leaving his party travelling around Italy like an unguided missile.

I have a photograph taken during Mr Whitlam's visit. It shows Mr Whitlam, Prime Minister Moro and our Ambassador, John Ryan. Fate can be cruel. We all know what happened to Mr Whitlam. Prime Minister Moro was shot by the Red Brigades some years later. John Ryan's career was ruined by his authorisation of the raid by ASIS on the Sheraton Hotel in Melbourne.

Ryan had been more active in administration in the Department than in policy matters and was greatly feared for his tight discipline of staff. He was often helpful to me, however, in the progress, such as it was, of my career. Those of us in the Embassy were grateful to him because he let us do what we wanted and pursue our own interests instead of dictating what should be done or what we should say or think. The Embassy worked better with this approach.

Italian reactions to Mr Whitlam's dismissal in November 1975 were interesting. They considered we had dealt with the crisis in a mature and decisive way. It was possibly in the back of their minds that anything like that in Italy would never have been settled but would have dragged on through the courts and elsewhere for years. There would have been countless conspiracy theories.

Another visitor of interest was Clyde Cameron, still a member of the House of Representatives, but no longer a minister. He spent several days in Rome and I accompanied him on his visits. I had heard of his penchant for plots and counterplots, but when he was in Rome he was most agreeable and seemed grateful for the arrangements we made for him. He entertained us greatly in the Roman restaurants at night with his reminiscences of political life in Australia. His published diaries give some account of his activities in Rome, particularly when we told him that the Whitlam Government had given us instructions on how to spell certain words – "program" instead of "programme", for example.

A visiting federal politician who had worked previously in the immigration section visited the Embassy and wanted to make contact with the Italo-Australians with whom he had worked. He summoned a meeting and began his oration by addressing them not as *concittadini* (fellow citizens) as he had intended, but as *contadini* (peasants).

Another visitor to Rome was Sir Zelman Cowen, not long before he was appointed Governor-General. He had been invited to a legal conference in northern Italy where he spoke about the dismissal of the Whitlam Government.

Sir Zelman was in Rome over Easter and expressed as desire to attend a midnight mass. I therefore took him on Easter Saturday night to the church of Santa Maria Maggiore where, it seemed, no mass was being celebrated. (I did not know then that, apparently, the Catholic Church does not hold a midnight mass on Easter Saturday.) We therefore went to the nearby Church of Santa Prassede, where a sign on the front door announced that the church was closed ("Chiuso"). While reading this sign, I became aware of a large cardboard container, like something that a refrigerator might be delivered in, next to the church. After a curious rustling noise was heard in the container, the top of it opened and a woman's head and upper torso emerged from it. "E chiuso" (it's closed), I said, pointing to the sign. "Si, e chiuso" replied the woman and Sir Zelman and I walked away. "Well, that's the weirdest conversation I have ever heard", said he. I ventured the opinion that the woman might be some kind of prostitute to which Sir Zelman replied "Well, if she is, she is plying her trade in a remarkable way, in a cardboard box outside Santa Prassede at midnight on Easter Saturday". He later said the episode was the strangest thing he had seen in Italy.

In Rome I lived in an apartment in the English College, an institution to which the English Catholic church had sent its candidates for the priesthood since, I think, the twelfth century. It was useful to have English-speaking landlords and the apartment, although of some antiquity, was pleasant and faced south. It was said to be haunted, but the ghosts only manifested themselves when there were children in the flat. As I had no children, I was not bothered by this apparition. But my successor, who did have children, told me that one night the ghost tried to get into bed with him.

The opera houses in Italy were a source of great pleasure to me, particularly La Scala, where the standard in those days was very high. In particular, the stage sets everywhere were often very beautiful, especially a *William Tell* I saw in Florence. There were some disappointments such as the atrocious settings for Wagner's *Ring of the Nibelung* in Milan. The conductor (Wolfgang Sawallisch) disapproved of them so much that he refused to conduct the final opera in the cycle. Sometimes I could fly to Venice on Friday, see a production in La Fenice that night, then go to Milan the next day for a matinee or an evening performance, then take the train to Turin on Sunday morning for a matinee there and return to Rome on Sunday night.

When asked what my favorite post was, I always answer "Rome", for obvious reasons. But of all the posts I had, Rome was the most difficult to live in on a day-by-day basis. Anything one did – cashing a cheque, posting a letter, having the car serviced, going to the dentist, seemed fraught with difficulties. Once an embassy officer who was doing the embassy's banking business was robbed. The surest way to ensure that a letter overseas reached its destination soon was to go to the Vatican and use its postal service. The Foreign Ministry often made appointments to receive us at 6 or 6.30 pm, which meant a long day. There was a shortage of small change in Italy in those days, and change was often given in the form of sweets or even boiled eggs.

An unexpected pleasure in Rome was skiing. It was possible to drive up to the Apennines, be there by 10.00 am, enjoy a few hours of skiing, and return to Rome before dark. One unexpected disappointment was the propensity of restaurants to serve food insufficiently hot.

7
BURMA, 1980-82
Before Aung San Suu Kyi

My first appointment as a head of a diplomatic mission was to Burma. The President of Burma was the dictator, General U Ne Win, whose twenty years rule had led to political, economic and social stagnation in Burma.

Our most important activity at the embassy in Rangoon was implementation of Australia's aid program. In 1980, when I arrived, this stood at A$8.5 million a year and ranked fifth amongst Australia's bilateral aid commitments, excluding Papua New Guinea; in 1981 it grew to nearly $A10 million. In general, the program was of high quality, successful and represented money well spent. Besides training and food assistance, Australia was committed to four projects, all of which I visited soon after arriving in Burma.

The most important was the Western Highway, a road building project, situated on the western side of the Irrawaddy River, undertaken by the Snowy Mountains Engineering Corporation as agents of the Australian Government. The purpose of the road was to open the country for the local inhabitants and also to serve a defence purpose, should the need ever arise. I have seldom visited such bleak and difficult country. The site of the road was about an hour's drive from the Irrawaddy. Until our road was built, there was no road at all in the area. During the monsoon the ground turned to mud. Even in the dry weather, the terrain was difficult. How the local people managed to take their produce to market or go anywhere I could not say. The first time I went there was in the middle of the hot season (April) and the temperature was said to

Richard Gate presenting credentials to President U Ne Win, Rangoon, 1980

be 110 F. at night. Tigers were not unknown in this country and, I regret to say, from a conservation of species point of view, that our hosts once procured some tiger meat for us. It had a nice, tangy, spicy taste. Very little of any kind of vegetation except poor scrub seemed to grow in this area which was, nevertheless, inhabited by thousands of brightly coloured birds. Visiting this part of the country made me realise how under-developed much of Burma was.

The second project was situated in the dry part of central Burma near the historic city of Pagan. Here, we provided tubewells in some 350 villages in order to bring them ready supplies of fresh water, thus making it unnecessary for villagers to trudge long distances carrying water in buckets. This project had significant implications for the long-term future of the villages. The main difficulties we experienced were in ensuring that the Burmese Government trained sufficient personnel in the maintenance of the pumps and in keeping them supplied with adequate quantities of diesel oil.

The third project, a small one, concerned irrigation in a remote area in Upper Burma. Here, the greatest difficulty we had was in selecting the right person for the job. The person concerned had to live full-time at the site and, being alone, was under the continual spotlight of local observation and bound by the considerable restraints of the strict Burmese code of moral and social behaviour. If the person concerned was not always able to adhere to these, it made administration of the project more difficult.

The fourth project, which fortunately was nearing a close when I arrived, was the provision of some grain silos for rice storage in central Burma. This project had been plagued for years by unsuitable equipment installed in the silos. It had damaged the rice which resulted in lower sales overseas and, hence, a decline in potential export earnings. Rectification of this project caused a number of headaches.

Our most important visitor was the then Deputy Prime Minister and Minister for Trade and Resources, J. D. Anthony, accompanied by fifteen Australian businessmen. Mr Anthony had long believed that there was scope for improvement in Australia's commercial relations with Burma, but the regime's reluctance to engage in joint ventures and its general suspicion of the commercial motives of foreigners meant that little resulted from the visit.

As Ambassador, I inherited one of the most famous residences in the Australian diplomatic service. The house itself, probably built in the 1920s, was not particularly distinguished architecturally or even comfortable; it faced south and was

Deputy Prime Minister and Minister for Trade and Resources, J. D. Anthony, at the Shwedagon Pagoda, Rangoon, 1982

subject to the full blast of the tropical sun all day. But it was situated in large, almost park-like grounds, with magnificent stands of trees (many of which were badly damaged many years later by a cyclone). The house was on higher ground than the rest of the compound; when I looked out of my window on the upper floor, I could not see any other houses, only tree-tops in my own garden. There was an excellent view of the Shwedagon Pagoda, Burma's most famous and most impressive structure, from the front of the house. At night, the gold-encrusted pagoda was illuminated.

During the war the Japanese army built a succession of caves under the house. After the war, these were filled in but, by that time, the caves had become infested with poisonous snakes. For years afterwards, these snakes continued to inhabit the house, to the extent that visitors were told that if they got up in the night they should on no account put their bare feet on the floor. Fortunately, by the time I arrived, the house had been made snake-proof and such incidents did not occur. The snakes had, apparently, deserted the compound entirely.

When I arrived in Burma in 1980, it was one of the few countries in South-East Asia to which Australians then had access which had not been seriously changed by modernisation and industrialisation. The then regime and the Burmese themselves had deliberately clung to their traditional ways and foreign influence in Burma was comparatively slight. Buddhism was probably even more firmly entrenched there than in Thailand or Sri Lanka. Burma had taken the South-East Asian penchant for neutrality and self-absorption further than any other country in the area.

Burma is topographically diverse – a plain surrounded on three sides by mountain ranges and by the sea on the fourth – and racially diverse. It includes not only the Burmans, but countless other groups such as the Karens, the Shans, the Mons, the Kachins and others (who together comprise the Burmese as distinct from the Burmans). Both these characteristics led to civil wars that have plagued the country's history, not least since independence. Burma is also a very rich country and, before the Second World War, its resources were profitably exploited. After independence, however, the continuing insurgency, the lack of technical know-how and the Ne Win Government's own backward economic policies prevented progressive exploitation of these resources. This was a great pity, as was the fact that so much of the country when I was there remained inaccessible to visitors because of the insurgency. The population in 1980 was slightly more than 33 million.

Despite its long history, there was surprisingly little evidence of the past in Burma. Apart from those in Pagan and elsewhere, most of the old buildings and monuments had been destroyed by fire, wars or the weather. Nor had the Burmans done much in recent times to develop and beautify their country. Rangoon itself and the basic infrastructure of the country were established by the British and not very much had been added to them since independence, mainly because of the continuing insurgency and the precarious economic condition that the country had been in since 1948. There were no great national museums in Burma, as there were in China, Japan and Korea and, in general, the Burmans did not seem to be very artistic. Traditional crafts such as lacquer and wood carving had been handed down and were still practised, but in more original and creative areas, such as painting, Burmese achievements now, and, as far as can be judged, in the past, are unimpressive. Nor, as far as I knew, was there much Burmese literature (although the literacy rate is high). Ne Win's regime did not encourage any creative writing, but I am not aware of any great earlier achievements.

Nor did the Burmese seem to have any gift for making their immediate surroundings look attractive, as do the Greeks for example. It was disappointing, when travelling in Burma, to notice how drab and ill-kept were the peasants' farms and villages, with collapsing bamboo fences everywhere. They contrasted badly with the trim little stone dwellings in Arab countries and the neat mud houses with thatched roofs that used to exist in Korea. With some exceptions, such as Meiktila, Maymyo and Kalaw, most Burmese towns were very similar and virtually indistinguishable from one another, and not particularly attractive. Usually the main centre of interest was a large pagoda. Some pagodas were pleasing to the eye, mainly when viewed from a distance, but most were garish and, to me, extremely ugly.

What was very surprising were the conditions in Burmese homes. Most Burmans seemed clean personally, but normal house cleaning or maintenance never seemed to be done. Everything was either dusty or grimy or covered with mould. It was not uncommon for individual Burmese to comment in a matter of fact voice that their homes were extremely dilapidated or even dirty, but nothing ever seemed to be done about it. Conditions in hospitals were unbelievable and were an indictment of the so-called socialist system under Ne Win, which reserved the best facilities for the elite.

Yet, despite all these considerations, most foreigners who have lived in Burma have enjoyed it and want to return. When I was posted to Bangladesh ten years after I had been in Burma, I went back to Rangoon once, or sometimes twice, in each of the four years I was in Dhaka. The main attractions of Burma are undoubtedly the beauty of the country, with an immense variety of scenery, and the charm and quality of the people. For one thing, the Burmans (at least those that diplomats are likely to meet) speak excellent English and, unlike others who speak tonal languages (such as the Thais and the Chinese), they speak it without the accent that makes the Thais so difficult to understand. Emphasis on English teaching decreased under Ne Win, but it was surprising how many young Burmese, who had not had as good a training in English as their parents, had managed to achieve an acceptable standard.

The Burmans also had a refreshing directness and frankness in dealing with foreigners that made them comparatively easy to associate with. They were not embarrassed or awkward in conversation with foreigners and many had an easy sense of humour. Like the Bangladeshis, they exhibited no sensitivity about race or colour, although they considered Burma to be the best place in the world and the Burmans the best people.

The distrust and disdain of foreigners that was a marked feature of the Ne Win regime was shared, to some extent, by many Burmans. The regime itself decreed, while I was there, that individuals from the headquarters of the Burma Socialist Program Party (then the ruling and only party) were prohibited from attending lectures by foreigners sponsored by embassies; the Party considered that it had nothing to learn from such contacts. The people themselves sometimes showed something of this trait. Despite the bad state of the Burmese economy, I never heard any Burmese admit, even privately, that Burma had anything to learn from any of the then recent Asian success stories in Taiwan, Japan or Korea. Their attitude to such countries was one of almost haughty indifference. When the UNDP Representative suggested to the Deputy Minister for Agriculture that Burma might be interested in a UN-sponsored nature conservation program, he was told that there was nothing in Buddhist teachings which required Burma to take an interest in the subject. It was said that when the Americans sent people to the moon, the Burmese Government claimed that Burmese had done that years ago.

The Burmese could also display a certain careful calculation that was, to say the least, disturbing. While I was there, a jilted suitor bribed a hairdresser to put a drugged poisonous snake in his former girl-friend's tresses as she was being coiffeured for her wedding. When the snake came to, after the wedding, as the girl was putting down her hair, it bit her and she died. During the more unsettled times of British rule, the Burmese used to settle scores with British officials by tying wires between two trees. The British cycling through the jungle would be decapitated.

Social life in Burma was puzzling. The regime did as much as it could to prevent contact between members of diplomatic missions and local people. All government officials had to seek permission to accept invitations to visit foreign missions. I had the impression, however, that people who really wanted to come were able to do so, but those who did not want to come seemed to invent difficulties that perhaps did not really exist. Certainly, the professional diplomats in the Foreign Ministry appeared to have little difficulty in accepting invitations, whereas the military officials who had been posted in the ministry seemed reluctant or unable to come. This may have been because the military officers were not on top of their portfolios and felt that they might be embarrassed by revealing their lack of knowledge.

There were alleged to be spies and informers all over the place, and no doubt there were, but I got to know more people well in Burma than I did in either Bangladesh or Jordan which were much more open societies. Maybe the difficulty of making friends somehow spurred the people to overcome them.

In recent years, long after leaving Burma, I have heard some Australian officers posted there express disappointment with the Burmese treatnent of the Rohingyas, even going so far as to claim that the Burmese were racists.

Travelling in Burma was difficult and exhausting. Even those areas where travel was permitted were difficult to penetrate because of the paucity of hotels, the poor condition of the roads, the difficulty of securing supplies of gasoline, the crowded conditions and frequent breakdowns of the railways and the erratic airline schedules.

The first time I visited the Western Highway Project, I expressed an interest in returning to Rangoon by train. This was duly organised, but it turned out to be a mistake. As the temperature at night had been 110, the temperature during the day in a non air-conditioned train can be barely imagined. For some reason, huge clouds of dust frequently blew into the carriage from the floor, giving us all uncontrollable coughing fits. Seated several seats ahead of me, and facing me, was an unfortunate young woman, attended by some friends, who seemed to be on the verge of dying. It was difficult (for me) to tell when we reached the end of the journey whether she was alive or not. All other members of our party, including the Burmese, were by that time exhausted and ill.

On another occasion, a group of ambassadors and their families, including myself, hired a railway carriage which was hitched onto a train and took us to Mandalay. This was highly enjoyable and we then took our cars into Upper Burma and visited, among other places, Kalaw. This town had been used as a "hill station" by the British to escape the heat of Rangoon. It was thickly covered with pine trees dotted amongst which were small English country houses in a state of disrepair but still habitable. The entire town was overrun with cuckoos whose constant calls, scattered throughout the pine trees, produced a delightfully stereophonic effect. Unfortunately, local inhabitants had developed the habit of cutting hunks out of the trunks of the pine trees to make charcoal and this had led to considerable ecological damage.

Mandalay itself, although little remains that is historic, is worth a visit as it gives some idea of Burma in pre-British days. It was the royal capital from 1857 until 1885 when the British conquered Burma. As the old royal capital, it was traditionally regarded by the Burmese as the primary symbol of sovereignty and identity. It suffered much damage under Japanese occupation during the Second World War. The old royal palace in the middle of town has disappeared but the huge grounds on which it was built have been preserved and some attempt has been made in recent years to rebuild parts of it, such as the gates and walls, as they must have existed in pre-colonial days. Now, however, the influx of Chinese residents has done much to alter the city's traditional appearance.

This trip to Upper Burma by the ambassadors occurred during

the Burmese "water festival" which takes place during the hottest part of summer. To get relief from the heat, the Burmese have developed the habit of hosing or throwing water at each other. Those travelling by car find it common to be inundated from buckets of water held by people travelling in the opposite direction. On this occasion, the British ambassador's sons and daughters left Kalaw to return to Rangoon (a journey of about two days). They had not gone far when they suddenly found themselves drenched and could do nothing to dry themselves (they had no fresh clothes) until they reached Rangoon the next day.

We also attended a famous "nat" (or spirit) festival in Upper Burma which is held annually. The nats are spirits who, I understand, although deriving from an earlier religion have somehow become mixed into Buddhism. It is said that "you worship the Buddha, but you fear the nats". When I broke my toe on two occasions in my own garden in Rangoon, some Burmese suggested I had offended the nats in the trees and bushes in the embassy compound. The particular festival we went to drew many people from all over Burma, partly because the particular nat being worshipped was believed to have curative powers. I was astonished at the number and variety of crippled or deformed people that appeared at the festival, some of them maimed in ways I could not have imagined or believed. In addition, they were extremely poor and with only rudimentary supports. The celebrations were noisy and excited and, at one stage, crammed into a small fenced area and, unable to get out, I thought I would be seriously injured.

The Foreign Ministry used occasionally to arrange trips for diplomats to visit parts of Burma. On one occasion we were taken to see the famous women of Padaung, a remote area of Upper Burma. The necks of these women had been greatly elongated as a result of the practice of putting a succession of metal rings around them, either (apparently) to prevent them being killed by tigers or escaping from their husbands. It is almost certainly true that if the metal rings were removed the women's necks would break immediately. The women showed us a copy of the *National Geographic* for 1950 which contained an article about them, with photographs. The curious thing was that the women we met (this was in 1982) looked exactly like the women in the 1950 photographs. They could not possibly have been the same, but we were unable to discover whether they were their daughters.

Flying in Burma was a unique experience. The planes always left Rangoon at about six or seven in the morning, so an early start was essential. The planes would not wait until all those who had purchased tickets arrived; as soon as they filled up they would leave, perhaps thirty minutes or so before the scheduled time. This made it impossible to know whether one would get away. An airline pilot told me that the planes were so dirty inside that they were hundreds of pounds overweight. The grime on the walls could be scraped off with a fingernail. Usually the door into the cockpit was left open, and it was obvious that the flying controls were covered with dust. This did little to restore confidence. On one occasion, the petrol started to stream out of the tank when the plane was airborne because the operator had not replaced the cap after filling the tank. The plane was forced to land on an island in the Irrawaddy River.

Burma became independent from British rule on 4 January 1948. Prior to that, nationalist movements had existed since the beginning of the century, but these were thrown into confusion by the Second World War. Some Burmese saw the Japanese as a useful means of ridding Burma of the British. Burma's national hero, Aung San (the father of Aung San Suu Kyi) and the "thirty comrades" (including Ne Win, the future dictator of Burma) went to Japan just before the war where they received military training under the Japanese on Hainan island. Aung San and others believed the Japanese would assist Burma in achieving independence.

As the war turned against the Japanese, some Burmese lost

confidence in them as being pro-independence and they called for temporary co-operation with the British. On March 1945, the Burma National Army rose up in a country-wide rebellion against the Japanese who were driven from Burma by May 1945. Negotiations with the British led eventually to independence on 4 January 1948. Aung San and his associates had won an overwhelming victory in elections for a constituent assembly in April,1947 but Aung San himself was assassinated in July. Burma elected to establish a republican form of government and was therefore not eligible to join the Commonwealth; at that time only "dominions"(that is, countries which recognised the British monarch as head of state) could join the Commonwealth.

Until the end of the 1950s Burma was governed by a parliamentary regime with, for most of the time, U Nu as Prime Minister. From what I know of U Nu's rule, it was not particularly efficient and certainly not free of corruption. U Nu himself was a famous "neutralist" figure on the world stage who, during his period in office, was almost as famous as other similar figures such as Nehru, Sukarno and Nasser. He was eventually overthrown early in the 1960s by the military regime headed by General Ne Win who later made himself President.

Partly because of the role the army believed it had played in achieving Burma's independence, it has always believed that it has a right to intervene, whenever necessary, in Burma's political affairs. Ne Win ruled until the late 1980s when, after a series of brief interim governments, he was replaced by another military regime. Unlike U Nu, Ne Win had no interest in cultivating any public image or in playing any leading role on the world stage.

During Ne Win's rule, virtually everything was run by the army, including the economy. All trade and industry was brought under state control with the top decisions being made by army officers. Most Burmese ambassadors were military officers who were under instructions to do virtually nothing. Almost all of these military officers lacked any kind of aptitude for their jobs and Burma gained very little, if anything, from their efforts. The dead hand of the army stifled initiative and frustrated the ambitions of talented people who could not aspire to the most senior positions. A general reluctance in the higher bureaucracy and ministry to take decisions led to elaborate and time-consuming systems of collective decision-making devised to spread responsibility for even the most mundane decision.

The main advantage, if it can be called that, of army rule was that Burma was spared the "development" that has taken place in other capital cities like Bangkok, Jakarta and Taipei, and which has turned those cities into polluted nightmares with never-ending traffic jams. In the 1980s and even the early 1990s Rangoon was still a leafy, attractive city in which it was easy to move around. Unfortunately, when I visited Burma in 2016, "development" had reared its ugly head in the form of multi-storied buildings erected in the most unsuitable places which spoiled the landscape.

During my initial round of courtesy calls in Rangoon, the Ambassador for Sri Lanka, speaking of Ne Win, said that he could not understand how "one man can keep an entire nation in absolute thraldom". I still have no answer to this puzzle. It is easy to say that Ne Win governed because he had the support of the army, but this simply begs the question as to how he was able to retain that support. He allowed no one to threaten or to rival him. His most trusted henchman during my time was Brigadier Tin Oo, head of the military security apparatus. Apart from Ne Win himself, Tin Oo was the most feared man in the country. Shortly after I left Burma, he was suddenly arrested and flung into prison where he languished for some years (and then, I believe, went blind).

Incidents like this were common in the Burma of that era, but the Burmese did not always take them as seriously as we would have done. Several well-known Burmese who had occupied positions of senior rank were in prison all the time I was in

Burma, having somehow incurred Ne Win's displeasure. I had the pleasure of meeting some when I returned to Rangoon during my later posting to Dhaka. They had by then been released from prison and had returned to the relaxing and convivial diplomatic cocktail/tennis round. Few seemed to be the worse for the time they had spent in prison, nor did they think it unnatural or unexpected that they should have been there.

Stories of Ne Win's ill-temper were legion. One very senior Burman, known, rightly, as "the father of the Burmese army", was one of Ne Win's regular golfing partners and told me it was quite common, when the game did not go Ne Win's way, for the President suddenly to attack his partners, beating them with his golf-sticks.

While I had been in Rome, I came to know a half-Burmese, half-Australian woman who was descended from the Burmese royal family. She had lived in Italy for many years, having been married for some time to an Italian. Ne Win frequently saw her when he came to Europe and eventually asked her to return to Burma and help him to modernise the country. The woman explained that she could not do this as Burmese laws inflicted heavy punishment on those who had left Burma and given up their citizenship. Ne Win acknowledged this and told the woman that the law could be circumvented if she married him and returned to Burma as his wife.

The woman did so and set up house-keeping with Ne Win in the presidential residence. But she found that, accustomed to modern Western life, she could not perform the role of the dutiful wife of an Oriental despot. Her efforts to "modernise" Burma infuriated Ne Win to the point that she found she had no option but to return for Italy. I was told he tried to strangle her. Ne Win thereupon returned to a more compliant wife whom he had abandoned several years earlier. I was warned in Burma not to mention that I had known this woman.

On another occasion, Ne Win, who lived beside a lake in the middle of Rangoon, became irritated by some dance music floating across the lake from a hotel. He jumped into his car, drove to the hotel, entered the dance hall and began attacking the musicians and their instruments, especially the drums. The musicians, not knowing who he was, started to fight back and were restrained only just before their actions would have landed them in serious trouble.

Although Ne Win wielded absolute power, this never seemed to involve him in the massive paper workload borne by political leaders in Western countries. His main concern was to keep his subordinates in order (at which task he was supreme), to outline general policies to be adopted and, by sudden visits and spot-checks, to make sure his instructions were obeyed. If these efforts were not enough, the frequent arbitrary arrests reminded everybody that he was in charge.

In view of what has been written about Burma since 1988 and the attention that Burma has attracted subsequently, it is important to emphasise that there was no democracy of any kind in Burma during the twenty-five years or so of Ne Win's rule. Ne Win ruled absolutely, both as President of the country and, later, after he had relinquished that position, as Chairman of the Burma Socialist Program Party. The so-called Parliament had no powers at all and simply did what it was told by Ne Win. Elections were rigged. The judicial system, although fair in some ways, had no independence from the Party. Nor was there any pretence that it, or anything else, should. The Constitution stated that the Party "shall lead the State".

There was no press freedom. All newspapers were published by the government and contained virtually no news at all. A leading headline would be "U Ne Win Gives Directives on Cement Mixing". Because of the regime's sensitivity, no news could be printed about, for example, the Soviet Union or the then current problems in Poland and other countries where communist dictatorships (on which U Ne Win's regime was modelled) were beginning to crumble. For one reason or another, virtually the only foreign news considered suitable for publication was from the Middle East. I profited from this anomaly when I was cross-posted to Jordan from Burma when my expertise gleaned from reading the Burmese press came in useful.

Other freedoms were denied in the most absurd way. All private organisations such as the Boy Scouts, the Lions, and the YMCA had been banned on the grounds that the state would take care of all matters traditionally looked after by such organisations. A mediocre Burmese Historical Society was eventually banned on the grounds that its activities might have been at variance with the state's interests. All private schools had been nationalised when Ne Win took power, with catastrophic results as far as the children were concerned. Books in the University library were locked up in case the students learned something new and interesting in them.

U Ne Win was, however, fairly scrupulous in permitting religious freedom. The Masons were allowed to continue on the grounds, either right or wrong, that Masonry was a religion. Ne Win did, however, interfere in religion to some extent, but only after careful consideration. He reformed the Buddhist clergy in 1980-81 when he established a nation-wide organisation of the priesthood, established religious courts, provided for registration of monks and for the expelling of corrupt or bogus monks from the priesthood. No other government in Burma had dared to do anything like this since the days of the Burmese kings. U Nu, U Ne Win's predecessor in the parliamentary regime, had unwisely mixed politics with religion and that had been one of the reasons for his downfall.

There was no economic freedom. All trading and manufacturing were undertaken by the state. The most that a private entrepreneur could do was to open a tea room, a laundry, a restaurant or a backyard plastics factory. Farming was distorted by demands that farmers supply rice to the government at artificially low prices.

The state industries produced little of value. Efforts were being made to produce a motor car, but I never saw the result and, in any case, its price would have been beyond the means of most Burmese. Anything of value that was traded was smuggled into the country from China or Thailand.

Ne Win and other Burmese of his age were brought up under the influence of institutions like the London School of Economics and the Indian independence movement. In their minds, capitalism and imperialism were inextricably linked. Ne Win therefore had a great suspicion of joint ventures with foreign companies which, he thought, represented a threat of control by a foreign, that is Western, government. There were very few, if any, joint ventures in Burma during my time. A few ventures were undertaken with foreign governments (such as the Japanese), but I do not recall that these amounted to much.

Checking on World Bank statistics when I was in Burma, I found the national economic indicators of Burma were, despite its vast natural resources, similar to those of such poor and small countries as Nepal and Laos. That this was the case was undoubtedly due to the anti-foreign, anti-private enterprise policy thrust on the country by Ne Win and inefficient management by the army. To some extent, this situation was mitigated by the fact that the people still had enough to eat because of the country's vast rice and fish harvest.

Very little of political consequence happened when I was in Burma. The early stages of Ne Win's rule, particularly in the 1960s and the early 1970s, had been unduly harsh, with many people thrown into prison. In June 1974, troops had been brought out to stop riots and demonstrations which broke out over food shortages, rising prices and bad labour conditions. Twenty-two people were killed, sixty injured and hundreds imprisoned. In

December 1974, further riots took place over the government's refusal to give U Thant an appropriate Buddhist burial. U Thant had been a famous Secretary-General of the United Nations and Ne Win was jealous of his international stature and did not like other Burmese playing a prominent role internationally. Again, troops were brought in, hundreds wounded, 4,500 arrested and many subsequently imprisoned. There were more riots in June 1975, leading to the arrest of 203 people.

By the time I arrived, conditions had eased somewhat. Most of those arrested in the early years of Ne Win's rule had been released. Foreigners were allowed into the country on a visa of seven days. Although the insurgency still raged in many areas, some travel was permitted. Economic conditions had improved slightly, particularly owing to the introduction of high yield varieties of rice. The regime itself felt more confident and had relaxed its grip a bit, although not much.

What was still absurd, however, was the way in which the regime tried to manage the details of Burmese life. All applications for passports and, I believe, permission to study abroad, had to be vetted by Cabinet. The Vice-President of the World Bank, chairing one of the annual meetings organised by the Bank for Burma and its aid donors, mentioned to the Burmese that the Government could not expect to be able to maintain this degree of oversight as the economy developed. The Government was offended by this advice and, rather than accept it, refused to allow any future meetings of the aid group to occur.

By 1981 Ne Win felt sufficiently confident to give up the presidency – he did not like having to meet ambassadors such as myself and other foreign visitors – to his old colleague, San Yu. I met San Yu several times, but he made no impression on me whatever. It was difficult to believe that he wielded any power and, probably, he did not do so as Ne Win continued to be in charge by retaining the presidency of the Burma Socialist

Program Party. San Yu, like all of Ne Win's other associates, disappeared from public life after the mass uprising and assumption of direct rule by the military in 1988.

Ne Win's departure from the presidency was preceded by eighteen months or so of efforts of "national reconciliation". These comprised the granting of amnesties to insurgents and the award of pensions and medals to old-time freedom fighters and other notables from the past. These were laudable enough actions at the time but they seemed not to have had much effect in the long run. Some had the opposite effect from what had been intended. Those who were to be awarded medals and pensions were on some occasions visited late at night by Ne Win's emissaries who had been directed to update the curriculum vitae of the individual concerned. The latter, however, only too well aware of what a late night visit from henchmen of U Ne Win entailed, immediately ordered their wives to prepare an overnight bag, expecting to spend the rest of the night in gaol.

But Ne Win's departure from the presidency did not make the future of Burmese politics any clearer. He had done nothing to groom any real successors and there was no one on the scene who had his personal force of character which, virtually by itself, enabled him to govern. Even in those days, however, continued rule by the army seemed the most likely prospect. Because of its place (whether justified or not) in leading the independence movement, the army had come to think of itself as the true guardian of the state. It honestly believed that if it disappeared, the state would collapse. The army had become, like the Communist Party in the old Soviet Union, a source of privilege. Those in the army enjoyed conditions denied to the great majority of Burmese. They had hospitals and other facilities which the ordinary Burmese never saw.

Part of the importance that the army attached to itself sprang from its role in defending the state against the insurgency that had plagued Burma since independence. Even during U Nu's parliamentary regime, the army's main task was to put down insurgency in the interests of a united Burma. In the field of counter-insurgency the army was one of the most experienced in the Far East. Although under Ne Win the army unfortunately became associated with maintenance of the regime and exclusion of its political opponents, its anti-insurgency task was legitimate, at least from the point of view of the Burmans. And the unpopular practices, such as impressment of civilians as porters for the army, date back to Ne Win's time.

No matter who was in power, Burma was governed after independence and under Ne Win by members of the same elite. The people whom Ne Win and his officers replaced in 1962 were not their worst enemies, but, in many cases, their best friends; Ne Win had been Chief of Staff of the army under U Nu. This is one reason why Aung San Suu Kyi at first terrified the military: she was a "foreigner" who had spent years outside Burma, was entirely unconnected with the traditional leadership (except for the important link provided by her father) but who had a direct appeal to the Burmese masses.

Where the early-post-Ne Win military regime (known as the SLORC) might have made some improvement was in the economic sphere, although I understand that much of this economic activity was financed by drug money. But the military permitted a degree of economic liberty that was unheard of in Ne Win's time. People were allowed to undertake economic ventures of their own and, in doing so, developed skills that could one day be of great benefit to Burma. One friend of mine, a former airline pilot, went into the oil business. He became a successful businessman and was able to travel abroad. Anything like that would have been absolutely prohibited under Ne Win.

The SLORC permitted Burmese with houses to let them to foreigners and receive rent in dollars which, to a degree, they were allowed to retain and use themselves. If they had enough money, they could travel abroad. In Ne Win's time, private travellers were allowed to take $40 with them, just about enough to get them into town from the Bangkok airport.

Finally, it is worth pointing out that Aung San Suu Kyi, even when she was under house arrest, represented an acknowledged rallying point for Burmese dissidents opposed to the SLORC. In Ne Win's time, no expression of dissent was permitted. A figure like Aung San Suu Kyi would not have been allowed to appear.

Like many other foreigners who lived in Burma, I became friendly with the former Chief Justice, U Myint Thein, who died in 1994 at the age of 95. Uncle Monty, as we called him, came from a brilliant Burmese family and had had a typically British colonial education (Cambridge, later called to the Bar). His family had had impeccable nationalist traditions during the agitation against British rule. He served as ambassador to China and as Chief Justice during the U Nu regime and, as far as I could appreciate, was world-class as a judge. As Chief Justice, he ranked second only to the Prime Minister of Burma in the Burmese hierarchy

U Myint Thein (Uncle Monty) and Richard Gate in Rangoon

and was therefore imprisoned by Ne Win after the latter seized power early in the 1960s. He remained in prison until 1968 during which period his wife died (there were no children).

Uncle Monty was one of the few people I knew who possessed almost perfect political insight and judgment. The Burmese political scene was in his blood, but his range of interests and grasp of affairs extended far beyond Burma. He pointed out to me, for example, when Britain went to war with Argentina over the Falkland Islands in 1982, that the Prime Minister of Israel, Begin, would take advantage of the diversion to mount an attack on Lebanon. This is exactly what happened.

When I was in Bangladesh I returned to Burma each year and saw Uncle Monty, then ninety. He was bedridden the last time I saw him in November 1993. Despite being almost completely blind and deaf, he remained amazingly sharp and well-informed. Only in one respect, I think, did his judgment falter. He could never accept that Aung San Suu Kyi had a legitimate place on the Burmese political scene. He could accept Ne Win, however much he disliked him, because Ne Win had been head of the army and had always been on stage. But Aung San Suu Kyi, whose parents Uncle Monty knew well, was an outsider, (as he called her) a "British house-wife". In this respect, Uncle Monty displayed the traditional Burmese suspicion of foreigners, or quasi-foreigners, playing a too prominent a role in Burma.

When I arrived in Rangoon, I found that there existed a sailing club on a small lake in the centre of the city. My father had been a good sailor, so I resolved to join the club and learn. This turned out to be a delightful experience and an excellent way of getting to know the Burmese, especially young people, on their home ground. They taught me to sail and I eventually participated, rather inexpertly, in races (I never won one until the day before I left Burma for Jordan). Several years after I left Burma, I unexpectedly received a letter informing me I had been awarded

Life Membership in the Club. When I went back, in 1993, more than ten years after leaving Burma, they gave me a dinner, attended by many children who had not even been born when I was posted in Rangoon, complete with such unusual refinements as table clothes and candlesticks. Almost all the young people I knew at the Club had left Burma to seek their fortunes in countries that offered greater opportunities.

8
JORDAN, 1982-85
At the Court of a King

I arrived in Jordan, from Burma, on 3 November 1982 as Australia's first resident ambassador. I remained until the end of 1985.

Jordan became an independent state in 1946, having previously been a protectorate under a mandate assigned by the League of Nations in 1922. First known as the Hashemite Kingdom of Transjordan, it was renamed the Hashemite Kingdom of Jordan in 1949 after gaining control of territories to the west of the Jordan River after the Arab-Israeli wars of 1948-9. It lost these territories to Israel after the 1967 war and renounced its claim to them in 1988, agreeing that the Palestine Liberation Movement (PLO) was "the sole legitimate representative of the Palestinian people". Emir Abdullah, the son of the Sharif Hussein of Mecca, became King of Transjordan in 1946. He was assassinated in 1951 and was succeeded by his son, Talal. He soon abdicated because of illness and was succeeded by his son, King Hussein, who ruled until his death in 1999. The succession passed to his son, King Abdullah II.

King Hussein had four wives. In the mid-1980s (when I was in Amman) his wife was Queen Noor (born Lisa Halaby in 1951), an American, the daughter of the Najeeb Halaby, of Syrian descent, who had been the head of Pan American World Airways before it went out of existence. She bore King Hussein four children. As far as I know, Queen Noor is still alive.

King Abdullah II is the son of King Hussein's second wife, Antoinette Gardiner, an Englishwoman.

The population of Jordan was estimated in 2015 to be about nine-and-a-half million, including about three million refugees, mostly from what is now Israel. This figure has been increased drastically in recent years by refugees from other Arab States, particularly Syria.

British influence remained in Jordan after independence; a British officer commanded the Jordan Army, known as the Arab Legion. However, in 1956, King Hussein arabised the army command and dismissed a number of British officers. Nevertheless, ties between Britain and Jordan are strong. While I was there both the Queen and the British Prime Minister, Mrs Thatcher, visited Amman. The British took their representation in Jordan seriously. One British ambassador, Sir John Coles, later became Permanent Under-Secretary of the Foreign and Commonwealth Office (and High Commissioner to Australia).

Before I arrived, Australia had had an Embassy in Jordan for a number of years, headed by a charge d'affaires. The ambassador had been resident in Syria. Several months before I arrived, the Department of Foreign Affairs had posted a new charge d'affaires on the understanding she would be there in that capacity as for a normal posting. Shortly after that, the Crown Prince of Jordan, Prince Hassan, visited Australia and, as a result of his representations, the Department agreed to post an ambassador. Because the Department knew that the charge d'affaires had expected to be charge for two or three years, it believed that if an ambassador who was on his first ambassadorial posting were sent there, an awkward personal situation between the two might arise. The Department decided, furthermore, that it would send an unmarried ambassador on the grounds, which seemed strange to me, that the wife of the ambassador might fight with the former charge d'affaires. These considerations seemed to lead inevitably to me.

Although I had hoped, after Burma, to go to a bigger, not a

smaller post, I was nevertheless willing to go to Jordan. The Middle East had always interested me and I wanted to see more of the historical and archaeological sites. In addition, President Reagan had recently launched an initiative which, he hoped, would lead to a settlement of the Israel-Arab dispute. Australia, too, had just agreed to participate in the Multinational Force and Observers monitoring the Israeli withdrawal from the Sinai desert, captured in the War of 1973. The Department told me that it therefore needed to be better informed on what was happening in the Middle East; hence the need for an ambassador in Jordan. All in all, it looked like an interesting posting.

To my surprise, I gradually became aware that Jordan had a slightly different concept of an ambassador from that which is normal. In most countries, any importance that an ambassador has derives from his position as the representative of another sovereign government. In Jordan, his importance derives from the fact that he is accredited to the Royal Court. Matters are therefore arranged to suit the convenience of the Court, not the ambassador. When the Court officials came to escort me to present my credentials, they did it in a manner that suggested I was an errant sheep being rounded up.

Partly because of this attitude, I did not present my credentials until three months after my arrival. The excuse was made that the King was too busy; he might well have been, but this excuse seemed rather lame when, eventually, arrangements were made for me to present credentials not to him, but to the Crown Prince. In any case, it is discourteous to make an ambassador wait so long. Our Australia Day reception had been held just several days before this ceremony took place, but, not having been officially accredited, I could not act as host. (This was not just a stuffy act of protocol; it would have been very offensive to my ambassadorial colleagues if I had assumed the role of an ambassador without first having presented my credentials.)

Richard Gate presenting credentials to Crown Prince Hassan of Jordan, Amman, 1983

It is usual for Heads of Mission, if they are being transferred from one post to another, to visit Australia en route to discuss their new posting with ministers and the Department. In this case, the Department suggested that, because I was the first ambassador, I should go directly to the post, see first hand what the circumstances were, and then go to Canberra to discuss them. Because of the delay in presenting credentials, I kept postponing the visit to Australia until, finally, after three months, the Department agreed that I should wait no longer and return to Australia anyway. Just at the last minute, before I was to leave, the presentation ceremony was arranged and I drove to the airport from the Royal Palace. This seemed a rather ludicrous beginning to my posting.

Because Heads of Mission cannot call on ministers until their credentials are presented, I could not begin my real work until I returned from Australia – about four months after first arriving at the post.

These events in some ways set the tone for my posting in Jordan. I did not find it easy, particularly at first, to secure access to ministers to discuss matters seriously with them. This was undoubtedly because the Jordanians did not consider that Australia was a major player in Middle Eastern affairs, or that it had any influence over what was being done there. It was also because events were shaped very much in the Royal Court and ministers and ministries were not always informed of what was happening. On several occasions early in my posting, I called on the Secretary for Foreign Affairs in order to ascertain his views on developments, but I learned absolutely nothing.

I did have one interview with the King. I was summoned to the palace suddenly at half an hour's notice. The King was very polite, as he always was, but it was clear that he was not telling me anything that I had not already heard in his TV and newspaper interviews. There was no reason why he should tell me his inmost thoughts; I was in no position to advance his interests. "The King has great personal charm and empathy," the British Ambassador remarked to me once. "After an audience with him, you feel much better". I did not feel much better after this interview with the King.

Heads of Mission were often summoned to a remote part of the country where the King was to officiate at the opening ceremony of a new forest or a new school. We would be asked to arrive at a particular time, but the King usually arrived forty five minutes after us. We would then be gathered into a particular area remote from the King who spoke only to his ministers or advisers. We wondered why we had been asked. Often the area into which we were ushered was so crowded I had doubts about our safety.

The King would not agree to see visiting Foreign Ministers or other dignitaries until they were in the country when his advisers would ask him if he would do so. Very often he did not and the Ministers were greatly offended, with grave effects on the ambassador. This never happened to me as the King was in Scotland when the Australian Foreign Minister, Mr Hayden, visited Jordan.

In my final eighteen months or two years I did enjoy access to the then Foreign Minister, Taher el-Masri, who was both well-informed and willing to talk frankly, and also to the then Prime Minister, Zaid Rifai. In part, this was because events involving Jordan and the PLO were gathering momentum and there was more to talk about. It was also because the visit by Mr Hayden had attracted their attention.

I learned much of what I came to know about the King's attitude to the Palestine problem from the United States and British ambassadors. The King thought aloud in their presence because he knew that their governments were influential in the Middle East. I do not think that these ambassadors ever released to me any very sensitive matters the King had mentioned to them, but they revealed enough to keep me well informed. Jordan is important to these countries.

The presence of many Palestinian refugees in Jordan inevitably led to speculation about the possibility of their destabilising the government. However, the Jordanians feared the PLO less than it did the other more extreme Palestinian organisations, some resident in Syria, who were bent on assassinations and other violent activities.

On the PLO side, I was able to establish a good relationship with Mohamed Milhem, the exiled mayor of a town on the West Bank, who was a member of the Executive Committee of the PLO. It was when I was in Jordan that Australian ambassadors were first allowed to establish contacts with members of the PLO. Mayor Milhem kept me well informed about the thinking of the higher echelons of the PLO. Later, he became reluctant to meet me in public places lest he be assassinated and worried that, if I visited him, I might be assassinated. We consequently saw less of each other.

On another occasion, I succeeded in getting an interview with another important PLO leader, Hani el-Hassan. He was also a member of the Palestine National Council and had been a PLO ambassador in a number of countries. After my only meeting he sent me a message to say that he did not want to see me again because the Australian Government was not prepared to invite him to Australia.

Faced with these kinds of problems, I came to see the truth in an observation made to me by another ambassador, that, although it was easy to find out the general drift of events in Jordan, it was very difficult to find out exactly what was happening. The same ambassador remarked that "if you are not a King, the King thinks you are a slave".

Australia's interests in Jordan were slight, but varied. We had a small aid program run by SAGRIC in South Australia devoted to improving dry-land farming. This was once described to me by the Minister for Agriculture as "a trivial thing". It was certainly difficult to impress its importance on visitors when all we had to show was a crop growing in a field.

As in other posts, the Head of Mission in Jordan had an amount of money to disperse to deserving institutions, such as schools or hospitals. In administering this "Head of Mission Discretionary Aid Fund" (HOMDAF), I always found, at whichever post I was, that the most difficult problem was to ensure that all the money was spent before the end of the financial year. There always seemed a tendency to let expenditure slip until the financial year had nearly ended.

Whenever the occasion arose for the equipment of an item supplied under HOMDAF to be handed over to the recipient institution, a small ceremony was usually arranged. I found that at these ceremonies in Jordan, Australia received very little credit for its contribution. Usually the leading figure at the ceremony would be a Jordanian dignitary, such as the Queen, and the publicity surrounding it would stress the Queen's commitment to the institution concerned and her unswerving support for it. The only reference to Australia would be that "the Australian Ambassador was also present." I was not the only Head of Mission who felt slightly put out by this treatment.

The Ambassador's Residence in Amman, 1982

Our exports to Jordan in 1984 amounted only to $A 13 million, although there were good prospects for sales of coal, wheat and steel. Sales of livestock and chilled meat were, as they still are, hampered by difficulties both in Australia and Jordan. The largest Australian business in Jordan was Grindlays Bank, which had been bought out by ANZ in 1984. At various times there were threats by the Jordanian Government to implement its requirement that 51 per cent of the Bank's shares be sold to Jordanians, but this did not happen, at least in my time. (In 2000, ANZ sold its Grindlays subsidiary to the Standard Chartered Bank.) Various other unusual proposals were made, such as one by the King Hussein Medical Center to buy in vitro fertilisation units from Australia and an offer by Mr R. J. L. Hawke to provide Industrial Safety Units to Jordan. These initiatives caused problems that were long in settling.

One of the most prestigious and visible activities of Australia in Jordan at that time was the archaeological dig at Pella, in the Jordan Valley, by a team from Sydney University under Professor Basil Hennessy and supported by the Australian National Gallery which published the team's findings. Pella proved to be one of the most rewarding excavations of the past forty years, with attested remains from the Lower Palaeolithic (c.1,200,000 years ago) to the late Medieval periods. I enjoyed visiting the team. Mr Hawke (by then Prime Minister) also visited them during his trip to Jordan after my departure, and he agreed to arrange for the team to receive a year's supply of Vegemite!

Professor Basil Hennessy and Dr Timothy Potts of Sydney University at the Australian archaeological dig at Pella, Jordan, 1984

King Hussein's Jordan was an impressive, well-governed Kingdom in many ways. Although much of the country is inhospitable desert, the government's writ ran everywhere and it was in firm control, a marked contrast to the situation in some African countries I had previously visited where I was on my own if I ventured out of town.

Despite security pre-occupations caused by Jordan's close proximity to Israel, the regime was unusually liberal, particularly in comparison with some other governments in the Middle East. Although the security service was ever-watchful, there were very few, if any, political prisoners. Travel was easy and foreign books and newspapers circulated freely, with only occasional censorship. The press was not particularly innovative or stimulating, but this often appeared more the result of the abilities and attitudes of journalists than of any government directive.

There was no parliament in Jordan when I arrived and no political parties were allowed. A parliament was restored, however, in 1984 after fresh elections. The King had believed, probably correctly, that the delicate balance of political forces which existed in Jordan and had been badly jarred by the struggles with Israel and the PLO in the 1960s and 1970s could have been seriously damaged by robust political life. One particular problem was that about two-thirds of the population were from Palestine. This group, if given the chance, might want to take unwise initiatives against Israel or to seize power in Jordan itself. The main result of the elections in 1984 seemed to be an increase in the influence of Islamic fundamentalists.

Economically, Jordan was not doing badly. It was supported largely by remittances from Jordanians working in the Gulf and elsewhere and also by subventions by the Arab oil states which felt an obligation to Jordan because it was a "frontline" state. These funds helped to compensate for Jordan's lack of natural resources. Economic policy was cautious and conservative. The Government avoided subsidies and other mistakes of many developing countries. Some Jordanians had become rich (in quite legitimate business activities) and Amman had an air of go-ahead prosperity

Much of my time was spent assessing the results of the "Reagan Initiative" – a plan outlined by President Reagan on TV on 1 September 1982 to make a fresh start in Middle East peace negotiations. President Reagan proposed a settlement of the Palestine problem that would mean self-government for the Palestinians in the West Bank and Gaza in association with Jordan. There would be a freeze on Israeli building activity in those areas. The final status of an undivided Jerusalem would be settled by negotiation.

President Reagan's initiative had a bad start when Israel, then under the Likud Government, rejected it two days after it had been announced. The Likud would not countenance any arrangement that returned the occupied territories to Arab sovereignty. The reaction of Arab governments differed: some were mildly interested; others, such as Syria, hostile. Nevertheless, the Arab League Summit, meeting in Fez in September 1982 (after the announcement of the Reagan Initiative) did propose a plan of its own (known as the Fez Plan) which marked a step forward in that it implicitly recognised Israel, something the Arabs had long been unwilling to do on their own initiative.

Though it ultimately collapsed, the most important development in the wake of the Reagan Initiative was the Agreement of 11 February 1985 between King Hussein and Arafat which called for total withdrawal from the territories occupied by Israel in 1967; the implementation of the right of self-determination for the Palestinian people which would be exercised "within the context of the formation of the proposed confederated Arab States of Jordan and Palestine"; and the resolution of the problem of the Palestine refugees in accordance with the United Nations resolutions. It called for an international conference to conduct peace negotiations to be attended by all five members of the Security Council and all parties to the conflict, including the PLO.

Throughout 1985, King Hussein continued to promote the 11 February Agreement and to urge, at the United Nations General Assembly and elsewhere, that an international conference take place at which a settlement would be reached on the basis of Resolution 242. The King implied that he had PLO acceptance of Resolution 242, with the recognition of Israel that it embodied.

The King was encouraged when, in his speech to the General Assembly on 21 October 1985, the new Prime Minister of Israel, Shimon Peres, cautiously endorsed the King's proposals. Shortly before this, Peres had made a statement to the Knesset in which he suggested for the first time the convening of an international peace conference.

Nevertheless, the 11 February Agreement came to nothing. The reasons were explained in detail to the Jordanian Parliament by the King in a speech on 19 February 1986, after his negotiations with Arafat had broken down. The main reason was that, despite the King's understanding, the PLO had ultimately refused to accept United Nations Security Council Reolution 242 which for years had been regarded as the keystone for a Middle East Peace Settlement, particularly by the United States, the key player in the whole process.

"Thus", the King said in his speech on 19 February 1986, "came to an end another chapter in the search for peace". Jordan was "unable to continue to co-ordinate politically with the PLO leadership until such time as their word becomes their bond, characterised by commitment, credibility and constancy."

It was not easy to follow or assess the significance of these developments. It was often difficult enough even to know what had happened. For example, the text of the 11 February Agreement was not made public until 24 February, almost two weeks after it had been signed. During this period, many governments, but not Australia, were asked to issue public statements in support of a document none of them had seen. As I had not seen it either, it was difficult to comment on it in reports to Canberra.

Assessment of other events was also difficult. Jordanian policy statements were sometimes difficult to reconcile with other facts. Jordan had joined with other Arab states in the Rabat Summit in 1974 in declaring that the PLO was the "sole legitimate representative of the Palestinian people". This Resolution was the origin of King Hussein's oft-repeated assertion that he could not speak for the Palestinians. It seemed anomalous therefore that there were seats in the Jordanian Parliament reserved for members from the West Bank.

On another occasion, Jordan amended its Constitution. I forget its nature but, according to the Government and the press, it constituted a milestone in development of Jordanian democracy. Conscious of the need to study a document of such importance, I asked several ministers and ministries to explain it to me and to send a copy. I never heard it satisfactorily explained and the copies that were sent were of a previous amendment. I never met anyone who had seen the actual amendment or knew what it said.

Partly because of the intractable nature of the Arab-Israeli dispute, Jordan seemed to have little interest in developments in other parts of the world. Fortunately I was never asked to make representations to the Foreign Ministry about international affairs that were of interest to Australia, and I do not believe that such representations would have interested the ministry. There was a small, private group called the World Affairs Council (or some such name) to which we would take visiting Australians to discuss international affairs. It was clear, however, that this group existed only to consider the Arab-Israel dispute and even discussing that was of little value as, the longer the discussion, the more bitter the members would gradually become at what they considered Western perfidy on that issue and the meeting would end on a rather sour note.

Some reflection of the crosscurrents at work amongst the

Arab States could be found in the attitudes of our own heads of mission in the area. No matter how well intentioned we all were, we were inevitably influenced by the perspective from which our host governments saw developments. Resident in Jordan, I naturally regarded the 11 February Agreement as a considerable step forward which showed some promise. My colleagues in other Arab states were dismissive because they believed that without the support of other Arab governments it could never be implemented. Our ambassadors in the Gulf states for their part attached more importance to the policy of their host governments, especially Saudi Arabia, whereas the Arab governments to the north regarded Saudi Arabia simply as a signer of cheques. "The Saudi Government has no foreign policy; it merely has an insurance policy," one senior Jordanian minister once said to me.

I left Jordan with some understanding of Israeli exasperation with the other side. The latter had missed many chances before the creation of Israel to arrive at some accommodation with the Jewish presence in Palestine. After the creation of Israel, the PLO launched a movement, which never had any chance of success, of eliminating Israel and recovering all of Palestine. After the Six Day War, when that objective became more remote than ever, it should have concentrated on recovering the West Bank and the Gaza Strip. Instead, it spent much time harping on the original injustice that had been done by the creation of Israel itself.

These were only the main mistakes of the Arab side. The others included, as I frequently observed, a failure to get its act together and to decide what it really wanted. Instead of approaching Israel itself, it wanted others, particularly the United States, to do it instead. There seemed to be a genuine inability or unwillingness to negotiate diplomatically. Just as the Israelis failed to see that the Palestinians had a case, the Palestinians and their supporters seemed never to understand that they were seen by Israel as constituting a genuine threat to that country. Nor did they realise, as President Sadat certainly had realised, that some genuine act

Canadian Ambassador Keith MacLellan, Richard Gate, HM the Queen, HRH Prince Philip, Indian Ambassador Santoshi, British Ambassador Sir Alan Urwick, Amman, 1984

was necessary to arrive at a solution. They expected Israel to make concessions that were not matched by any spectacular shows of compromise on their side.

As I look back, it now seems that I enjoyed my time in Israel more than my time in Jordan. Perhaps that was because I was younger, but I think it was also because Israel provided a more stimulating environment.

Australia is too remote from the Middle East to make any serious, major contribution to a settlement there. The concepts in international relations that prevail there are different from those that we hold. Nor does it seem easy even for Australian ministers to travel so far. As explained above, Sir Robert Menzies's visit to Israel was cancelled at the last moment. Later, Deputy Prime Minister J.D. Anthony was planning a visit to Jordan during my first few months in Amman, but had to give up the attempt when the Fraser Government was defeated in March 1983. Foreign Minister A.A. Street had also planned a visit, which was abandoned when he had to return home to vote in a Liberal Party leadership contest. Foreign Minister W.G. Hayden (later Governor-General) did visit Jordan during my time; his visit was cut short by the death of his mother and he only stayed a day and a half.

Queen Elizabeth II visited Jordan during my posting. Along with other Heads of Mission, I met her at the airport, attended various functions and was photographed with her together with other Commonwealth Heads of Mission. I met her four times but, although she seemed pleased to learn who I was, she said nothing to me.

Malcolm Fraser made a personal visit to Jordan after losing office. King Hussein had visited Australia when Fraser was Prime Minister and the King had invited him back. I would have thought that the invitation was meant to apply while Mr Fraser was Prime Minister, but he came anyway. I was absent from Amman at the time at a Heads of Mission Conference in Cairo. He saw the King and various other people but swore the Embassy to secrecy about his visit and forbade them to mention the details to anyone, even to me. I am unable to report anything about it.

I returned to Canberra after Jordan without knowing what was to happen to me. After some weeks in Canberra, I was offered the post of Deputy High Commissioner in New Zealand and I accepted it.

9

NEW ZEALAND, 1986-88

A Degree of Estrangement

The following exchange took place in the breakfast room of a Canberra hotel in the 1970s between the Australian High Commissioner to New Zealand and a senior official from the New Zealand Foreign Ministry. They, and some other New Zealand officials, had come to Canberra for discussions with officials of the Australian Department of Foreign Affairs. The previous day they had issued a communique:

> New Zealand official: I see there's nothing in your newspaper today about our communique yesterday.
>
> Australian High Commissioner (whipping out a copy of the *Canberra Times)*: There is. Look here. It's right here. See?
>
> New Zealand official: Well, what sort of hotel is this anyway? If you stay in the James Cook Hotel in Wellington you get a copy of *The Dominion* put under your door each morning.
>
> Australian High Commissioner: The James Cook? I wouldn't be caught dead in that dump. *The Dominion*? I wouldn't read that rag if you paid me.

These observations reflect attitudes that were once not uncommon on both sides. I think it is fair to say that in recent years relations between Australian and New Zealand officials have become much friendlier.

I arrived in Wellington in mid-1986. The High Commissioner was Mr L. R. Johnson, a former Minister for Housing (later Housing and Construction) and subsequently Minister for Aboriginal Affairs in the Whitlam Government. He was one of the few ministers in that government to escape controversy. After Labor was returned to office in 1983 he was appointed Deputy Speaker in the House of Representatives. Mr Johnson had an acute political sense and a great deal of common sense. He was not a fanatic of either the right wing or the left wing in the Labor Party, although I think his true heart was in the right wing. He did not particularly enjoy his time in New Zealand, citing as one of his complaints the poor quality, as he saw them, of the small goods. His judgment of New Zealand affairs was excellent and he had a wide range of contacts.

Professor (now Dame) Margaret Clark, Political Science Department, Victoria University, Merwyn Norrish, Secretary of Foreign Affairs, and Dr R. S. (later Sir Roderick) Deane, Chief Executive of the Electricity Corporation, Wellington

It makes sense to have a former Federal politician as High Commissioner to New Zealand. The New Zealanders are intensely interested in many aspects of public life in Australia and often have complaints about it. A politician with experience in Cabinet is likely to be able to answer the New Zealanders' questions and complaints better than a public servant who does not have the same experience of public life in Australia. One non-politician who was High Commissioner in New Zealand confided to me: "I can usually answer the first question, but not subsequent ones."

When I went to New Zealand, the New Zealand Labor Government, led by Prime Minister David Lange, had recently declared that it would not welcome into its ports any American naval vessels that carried nuclear weapons. As the United States refused to state whether any particular ship did or did not carry nuclear weapons, this meant that no American naval vessels entered New Zealand ports during the course of their routine operations in the Pacific. Under the influence of Helen Clark and other politicians, the anti-nuclear policy seemed almost to have become a national religion which it was treasonable to question.

The Hawke Government declared that it disagreed completely with New Zealand policy in this regard but that we were not prepared to be an intermediary or carry messages between the American and New Zealand governments. This had a deleterious effect on the operations of the tripartite ANZUS Treaty signed in 1951. The situation deteriorated sometime after I arrived in New Zealand when the United States, irritated by a statement by Prime Minister Lange, withdrew its security guarantee to New Zealand. This meant that New Zealand was thenceforth excluded from ANZUS Council meetings which subsequently took place between Australia and the United States.

My job in New Zealand was to report on New Zealand policies and actions relevant to these matters. The High Commissioner had excellent contacts and I was able to weave what he was told by New Zealand ministers and officials into my reports. At no stage, however, did we receive any instructions from Canberra to make any formal objections to New Zealand's policy. At least two Australian ministers visited New Zealand while I was there, Prime Minister Hawke and Foreign Minister Hayden, but I did not hear them raise any objections to New Zealand's policy.

In one way, we had more problems about the nuclear policy with the Americans in New Zealand than we did with the New Zealanders. Sometimes the American Ambassador would draw me aside at cocktail parties and claim that Australia was two-faced about this matter. He said that, while we declared we were opposed to New Zealand's policy, we were cuddling up to New Zealand in many other ways. I explained to him, as he should have known already, that Australia had a close relationship with New Zealand on many matters such as trade, health, education, science, agriculture, and civil aviation and that these matters required close and constant consultation and could not be brushed aside just because of New Zealand's nuclear policy. We gathered from our Embassy in Washington, however, that officials there did not share the American Ambassador's view.

There was considerable division in New Zealand over the anti-nuclear policy. At one stage, a senior Australian official visited New Zealand for talks with ministers and officials. I accompanied him on his calls and we were astonished at the degree of hostility there was amongst senior officials and service personnel to the anti-nuclear policy.

David Lange was not especially impressive. He was undoubtedly chosen for the job because his quick wit made him the only person who could outmanoeuvre his predecessor, Robert Muldoon, in Parliament. Lange's background was that of a small-time lawyer and he lacked the education, background and experience to be prime minister of an advanced country like New Zealand. I gathered many New Zealanders shared my view and I am not sure that New Zealand has recovered from the damaging effects in its international relations during his prime ministership. Lange had little experience of or interest in international relations. As a result of his policies, the ANZUS Council no longer meets and the United States has not reintroduced its security guarantee to New Zealand. In the post-Cold War world, that may not be as important as it was in the 1980s.

At one time it became known that Lange was anxious to visit a number of countries in Europe, Asia and the Pacific. Word gradually came back that he was not wanted in any of them. The Japanese gave the excuse that their ministers were too busy with tax reform to see him and other countries gave other excuses. It was clear that his policies had not won him much support overseas

A curious episode involving the Soviet Ambassador (I forget the details) attracted some attention. I asked whether we could have an explanation and received a reply that the Prime Minister would brief me about it, but not the High Commissioner. I did not inform the High Commissioner of this, but told the New Zealanders that I did not think this was the correct way to proceed and dropped the matter.

I greatly enjoyed my time in Wellington. I made many friends and I found New Zealand ministers and officials at all time friendly and helpful. I cannot say that I found much, if any, evidence of the resentment of Australia that New Zealanders are often said to show. Occasionally, there was an outburst of anti-Australian feeling amongst the public over something like a sporting fixture but, on the whole, leading New Zealanders knew that it was in their interest to work with Australia and to make relations as smooth as possible.

It was also a pleasure to be in a city where I could walk up the street and get my dry cleaning done, post a letter, get money from the bank, go to the dentist, have a cup of coffee and do other things that had not been easy in Burma or Jordan or even, sometimes, Italy. I had a very comfortable residence in the suburb of Khandallah overlooking the harbour. The ground below it slipped away and the house was supported by two long and sturdy spikes. There was always the risk that the house might be severely damaged by an earthquake and I understand it has now been sold.

I took a Master's degree in Political Science at Victoria University in Wellington. The subject was the Reagan Initiative – the effort in 1982 by President Reagan to secure peace between Israel and the Palestinians. I had amassed a good deal of material on this when I was in Jordan and wanted to do something with it. Professor (now Dame) Margaret Clark of the Political Science Department of Victoria University was most helpful. The wife of a senior New Zealand public servant, she had none of the hostility towards diplomats and other public servants that academics sometimes show. The whole exercise turned out to be a good public relations exercise and enabled me to enter academic and other circles in Wellington.

Life in New Zealand is very similar to life in Australia, but there are some differences. Many Wellingtonians have weekend houses on the Kapiti Coast which they refer to as "baches". I was sometimes invited to one of these houses for lunch, a drive of a little over an hour. While this made for a pleasant outing, I could never understand the purpose of these "baches". The houses were usually not as nice as the owner's house in Wellington and there was nothing to do there except walk on the beach. The water was too cold to swim in (it was often too cold to go outside) and the beaches were stony and unattractive. Life in a "bach" seemed rather purposeless.

The interior of the houses was also different. Many had wallpaper and I understand that the prevalence of wallpaper was in some way related to earthquakes, but it gave the houses an old-fashioned look. Where many Australian houses are festooned with ubiquitous gum tree art, the equivalent in New Zealand seemed to be small pictures of very brightly coloured English gardens. And, again unlike Australia, the telephone books contained dramatic instructions about what to do in the event of a tidal wave, an earthquake or a volcanic eruption.

We had many visitors to New Zealand. The most important

Richard Gate at the Agrodome, Rotorua, 1987

was that of Prime Minister Hawke, and his wife, Hazel. Mr Hawke had created a particular public personality for himself over the years, but in New Zealand both he and his wife were the very models of well-behaved visitors – courteous, patient, good listeners and interested in everything they saw and everyone they met. Their patience must have been tested when a plane crashed into some power lines outside Wellington and cut off the power supply to their hotel.

New Zealanders are well-informed generally about cultural life in Australia and any Australian artistic product of good quality will be well-received. Visits by groups such as the Australia Ensemble and other chamber music groups were very successful. Sometime later, prior to one of the New Zealand Festivals, the Prime Minister, Helen Clark, came to Australia and asked the

National Gallery to send over the paintings by Sydney Nolan of the Ned Kelly legend for the Festival. The Gallery could hardly refuse the Prime Minister's request and the paintings were popular in Wellington.

10
BANGLADESH, 1989-93
An Unexpected Revolution

Before leaving Wellington, I was informed that I was to be posted as Ambassador to Syria. After I returned to Canberra, I spent weeks waiting for the Syrians to agree to the appointment. Eventually, word came back that the appointment was unacceptable because I had been in Israel, a country with which Syria was at war. I therefore worked on Pacific affairs for a year until I was posted to Bangladesh as High Commissioner.

Bangladesh was my last and longest post in the Australian Foreign Service. I arrived in the capital, Dhaka, on 31 October 1989 and left on 2 November 1993.

In some ways, Bangladesh was the most satisfying of my Head of Mission appointments. As I was there for four years, I came to know the politics and economics of the country well; in Burma, when I left after two and half years, I felt I had only just begun to know it. My posting to Dhaka was eventful, as the following account will make clear. After Jordan, it was a relief to be in a country where Australia was fairly well known and where we counted for something.

The first Australian High Commissioner in Bangladesh, Jim Allen, was specially remembered because he had been sympathetic to Bangladeshi independence at the time of the war against Pakistan in 1971-72 and because he spoke Bengali (having been brought up in a missionary family in Bengal). Many Bangladeshis who had been overseas at the time of independence in Pakistani diplomatic missions and other jobs had been helped by Australians when they defected from Pakistan and were left virtually helpless. R.G. Casey was still remembered by older Bengalis for his role as Governor of Bengal at the end of the Second World War.

Again, unlike Jordan, we had been established in Bangladesh for many years and had an excellent office which we had built to our own design and to meet our own requirements. The residence, although not ideal, was satisfactory. Last, and certainly not least, I found a helpful and competent staff in Dhaka.

Bangladesh and Burma are contiguous and share many similarities. Flora and fauna are very similar and it was a pleasure to hear again the birds I had heard in my garden in Rangoon. The basic ingredients of the food are the same, although cuisine differed widely. As in Burma, the pork was excellent, but in Bangladesh we could not serve it when entertaining the Islamic Bengalis. Shell fish, as in Burma, were also excellent. On the whole, however, I found Bangladesh food no more palatable than Burmese food. It was almost always the same – lamb curry, fish curry and chicken curry, with rice. I daresay I should have been grateful to be able to eat anything when so many Bangladeshis were starving, but that virtuous thought did not make the food any more agreeable. The climate in Bangladesh was less oppressively tropical than in Burma and there were four months of the year – from November to February – when the climate was temperate and one could walk about without breaking out into a sweat. Often in winter it was cold and elderly, poor Bangladeshis in the north would die from exposure.

Bangladesh was my only posting in the sub-continent. I was able to make two trips to India to see the historical and archaeological sites in India, but there was comparatively little to see in Bangladesh itself.

Travelling in Bangladesh in some ways was more difficult than travel in Burma. We usually avoided going in the very hot weather (March-May) or the monsoon season (June-October). However,

Richard Gate presenting credentials to President Ershad in Dhaka, 1989

as soon as the weather became more agreeable, the pleasanter months were filled with political demonstrations more or less continually throughout the country. I had to cancel my planned trip to the north-west on four different occasions. The roads were so bad that when I was invited to visit people who lived only forty or fifty miles away subsequent research often revealed that it would take six or seven hours to reach them. The result of all this was that I travelled only during two of the four winters I was in Bangladesh.

One of the most alarming experiences was to cross one of the gigantic rivers on a car ferry. Dozens of buses, trucks and cars would be crowded on board, not to mention hundreds of people. No matter how many vehicles and people were already squeezed in, there were always many, many more being loaded. The traffic itself on the main road was often frightening. The trucks and buses, many of them old and dilapidated and moving crabwise, went at a reckless pace along narrow and raised roads between paddy fields, blaring music from a loud speaker on top. There were many accidents. I even found going the short distance from Dhaka to the airport a worrying experience as it meant travelling along the main north-south road for about five minutes.

There were four main areas of interest. The Chittagong Hill Tracts (CHT) in the south-east offered a change from the universally flat character of the landscape in the rest of Bangladesh and the scenery was beautiful. Unfortunately, the unrest in the CHT caused by influx of Moslem settlers from elsewhere in Bangladesh and the displacement of the native tribes made the area comparatively unsafe for travellers. I only managed one trip there.

The hilly areas in the north-east of Bangladesh, in Sylhet, are notable for tea plantations. I likewise visited this area only once, during a monsoon; as much of the surrounding country was flooded, it was not easy to gain much of an impression of the region. Members of an Australian family from Dhaka later visited Sylhet and were all nearly killed when their car was hit by a train at a level crossing in one of the tea plantations.

The area in the Ganges Delta, known as the Sundarbans, in the south-west, bordering on India, is unsuited for human habitation and remains the haunt of the Bengal tiger. I visited this area once on a ship belonging to the forestry department. We saw no tigers and the overall impression was one of gloom and impenetrability.

The most enjoyable trip I made was to the north-west, near Rajshahi and Rangpur. Here the country is drier and more hospitable, with long vistas.

On another occasion, shortly after my arrival, I visited a hospital established and run by Australian Baptists in the north, near the Indian border. I was very impressed with the work the Australians were doing there, in very difficult circumstances. I remember seeing one old man whose legs had had to be removed because they had become gangrenous as a result of smoking too much (this situation is common in Bangladesh; the local cigarettes seem

The gradual inundation of the island of Bhola

to be particularly lethal). As he could not work and had no family, his future would be on the streets, begging. An old woman had had breast cancer and had neglected it for so long that her breasts had become worm-infested and fly-blown. The doctor could do nothing for her and explained to me that she would probably die the next day. One young patient had a piece of sticking plaster stuck on his forehead. The doctor explained that the patient had a headache and thought that the sticking plaster would draw the headache out. In all the circumstances, I was amazed that the doctor had been able to accomplish anything.

My last trip was to the island of Bhola, right at the tip of the delta in the south, where I was taken by the local member of Parliament, Tofail Ahmed. Because the river had changed its course during the previous 45 years, much of this island has been gradually eaten away and subsequently disappeared. Many of the islanders, who were poor enough to begin with, had consequently lost all their land. The river does not suddenly break off huge chunks of land, but, rather, the water table rises until it gradually appears above the surface of the ground. First the ground itself disappears, then bushes, then houses and eventually trees. The sight of the beginnings of this development, with pools of water everywhere, is unnerving and destabilising in the extreme.

To get to Bhola we travelled on a large steamer that regularly conveyed travellers down the rivers. It was pleasant to sit on the decks and watch the sun set and the river come to life at night. We arrived at our destination at four in the morning and, although we did not disembark until about eight o'clock, the din of disembarking passengers and unloading of goods meant that any further sleep was impossible after the ship tied up at the wharf.

Social life in Bangladesh was very different from that in Burma. In the latter country the government put as many barriers as it could between the Burmese and foreigners, but individual Burmese would find ways to circumvent these restrictions and life-long friendships with foreigners were formed. There were no such restrictions in Bangladesh, but somehow close relations did not eventuate. As in Jordan, the Bangladeshis gave enormous parties to which everybody they had ever spoken to would be invited. While enjoyable and providing a useful way of making contacts, these events seemed to lack the degree of intimacy that they had in Burma. They were made tiring for me by the Bengali guests' custom of arriving at least an hour late and the hosts' custom of not serving the dinner until ten o'clock at the earliest, by which time I was hungry and exhausted.

The foreign community was unexpectedly large, mostly because the serious problems that Bangladesh faced attracted many foreign organisations such as the United Nations Development Program, the World Bank, the World Health Organization, the Asia Foundation, the Ford Foundation and others. Among the Australians were the Snowy Mountains Engineering Corporation and John Holland Pty Ltd which did work for the Bangladesh Government, and an assortment of religious bodies.

BANGLADESH, 1989-93

Many Australians who come to Bangladesh are shocked by the poverty. As I had been in places like India and Egypt I was perhaps not so shocked as many others and was quite touched by the apparent happiness of many people, particularly children, living in conditions of complete squalor in and around Dhaka. But I had never been in such a crowded country. Even in rural areas, it was impossible to get away from people. If the car broke down, in no time we would be surrounded by about two to three hundred people who emerged from nowhere. The old Australian practice of "going behind a tree" is impossible in Bangladesh; there are always two or three people behind the tree already. The centre of Dhaka was so overcrowded that it was almost impossible to take a car there. Huge throngs constantly surrounded the airport making ingress and egress difficult. Blind, maimed and crippled beggars held up cars at every intersection in Dhaka. As it took 30 minutes to get from the office to the Foreign Ministry, one hour was lost in travelling time for each appointment.

It was amazing that, under these circumstances, the country held together. The great mass of the people accepted some kind of discipline, perhaps Islam, that kept them from breaking out of control. Many Bangladeshis and some foreigners predicted that this state of affairs would not last forever and eventually it would be impossible for foreigners to venture downtown; the degree of resentment against their privileged status would be too great and their lives and property would be in danger.

I had a chance to observe the resilience of the Bangladeshi people in the aftermath of the great cyclone which hit the country in March 1991 when nearly 150,000 people were killed. The area worst hit was around Chittagong and some of the islands in the Bay of Bengal. Many homes were destroyed and much damage was done to crops. I flew over some of the affected islands a few weeks after the cyclone. For some reason, the Government had assigned me as co-passenger to Signora Fanfani, wife of a former Prime Minister of Italy. Signora Fanfani proposed countless and wildly impractical initiatives which Australia and Italy might take to ameliorate the plight of those stricken by the cyclone. Eventually, her companion, another Italian woman, whispered to me, "don't worry, you'll never hear anything more about all this", and I never did. The plane flew low and the people on the ground rushed out from their shelters and made imploring gestures in the hope that we would drop food and supplies. With assistance from the Government, international aid agencies and an American naval task force which happened to be in the area returning from Iraq, Bangladesh did recover and the long-term damage was manageable, apart from the almost total destruction of the Bangladeshi Air Force which was stationed on the ground at Chittagong.

Australia contributed to the relief effort, but this was not easy to organise. The transmitter south of Chittagong which cabled our telegrams to Canberra was blown down in the cyclone and we remained incommunicado for more than a week. Neither did the telephones work. I finally managed to get the French Ambassador, whose transmitter had remained erect, to send a cable to his Embassy in Canberra, for on-forwarding to the Department of Foreign Affairs and Trade, explaining our situation. I learned when I visited Canberra some months later that the relevant political section in the Department had not even noticed that they were not receiving messages from us.

Bengal was the area of India conquered first by the British, in 1757 at the Battle of Plassey, and the Bengalis were therefore the first inhabitants of the sub-continent to be exposed to British rule. Many remnants of this long exposure are still evident including a peculiar brand of English, manifest now mainly in the press. Newspapers are full of sentences such as "the miscreants crept into the house in the dead of night with deadly weapons"; or "the miscreants who did the deadly deed are now absconding". People never died; they always "expired". A politician never called for something; he "issued a clarion call".

Although I had never served in India, I had always been told by those who had that Indians were extremely sensitive on racial questions. I had expected to find the same in Bangladesh but, on the whole, Bengalis were not especially sensitive on this point, any more than the Burmese had been.

The substantive matters in Australia's relations with Bangladesh in the early 1990s were mainly concerned with immigration, trade, the aid program of about $A20 million per year and human rights questions.

Although some Bangladeshis remembered Australia's role at the time of its independence, political relations between the two countries were slight. On one occasion I was asked to inform the Government of a general liberalisation of Australia's trade policies which made it easier for Bangladesh to export to Australia. Far from being grateful, Bangladesh immediately asked for more concessions. For this and other reasons I was not anxious to raise Australia's profile. The only occasion when a matter of substance was raised with me was when a senior officer in the Foreign Ministry said he had heard that Australia might leave the Commonwealth. I explained that this was not the case. The Prime Minister (Paul Keating) had raised the possibility of Australia becoming a republic, but within the Commonwealth, just like Bangladesh. At the mention of Keating's name, the official's face clouded over and he said, "but he touched the monarch". This was a reference to the occasion when Keating had either put his arm around the Queen or touched her arm at a reception at Parliament House in Canberra. The official seemed to think this was a most unseemly gesture.

Our immigration policy was the same as in other countries. If Bangladeshis met the criteria, they would be given a migrant visa. Many could not meet the criteria and consequently those who were given visitor visas tended to overstay in Australia and tried to become permanent residents; at one stage, Bangladeshis constituted the largest number of over-stayers in Australia. At another time, I was told that 400 Bangladeshis had applied for refugee status in Australia, a figure much, much higher than the number who genuinely deserved refugee status possibly could be.

There was keen interest amongst Bangladeshis in getting a visa to Australia. On one occasion, an enterprising individual got hold of a visa information paper from our office and, after duplicating it, sold thousands to potential migrants at the railway station. (The document was supplied free by the High Commission.) So many people filled in this form, thinking that it would open the migration gate to them, and sent it to us that we filled 26 mail bags with them. These documents threatened to engulf the High Commission. Although it was our policy to answer each applicant, in the end I had to order that the documents be destroyed after rats had nested in the 26 mail bags, creating a health hazard. Even disposing of the bags and the documents was a mammoth task.

Two-way trade reached about $A100 million during the early 1990s, with Australian exports reaching about $A70 million. This was a healthy sum, at the time, more than our exports to the Indo-Chinese countries or, for example, to Mexico and Israel.

Most Australian aid, which totalled about $20 million a year, was devoted to provision of food. This was distributed to the poor as payment for their work on construction projects throughout the country or, in other areas, to women in return for their promising to enrol themselves in literacy classes and other income-generating activities. In general, this aid reached its beneficiaries more quickly than it would have if it had been spent on massive "projects" such as building of bridges or dams. Our only "visible" project aid was concessional financial assistance to construction of a hangar for repair of aircraft; the work was undertaken by John Holland. Other aid, often provided through international agencies such as the World Food Program, went to the population and health sector, with particular reference to contraception and immunisation, assistance after the great cyclone of 1991, aid to Rohingya refugees, Bangladeshi non-governmental organisations and about 40 scholarships a year for study in Australia. In these areas, too, the beneficiaries were quick to see results.

Political Life

Political life was eventful and I became more of a participant in it than I had expected. There was much sympathy for Bangladesh when it broke away from Pakistan in the 1970s and it had a fairly good start as an independent nation. Unfortunately, its unstable political development since those days has shattered its image. Once, when I spoke to the Foreign Secretary about human rights in neighbouring Burma, he explained that Bangladesh was unable to take any prominent public role in such discussions as Bangladesh, as a result of its history of coups and dictatorships, had no credibility on this score.

President Ershad, a former army general, who was in power when I arrived in Dhaka, had been in control since he staged a coup in 1982. Personally, Ershad was approachable and easy to deal with. The ceremony at which I presented my credentials was unusual in that, for the first time in my experience, I had several substantial matters I wanted to discuss with the Head of State. Usually, these ceremonies are devoted to pleasantries or general statements about the excellent state of relations that exist (or are supposed to exist) between the two countries.

This time, however, I wanted to raise the case of an Australian citizen (a Jew born in Israel) who was subject to persecution by the Bangladesh administration. I was seeking some kind of guarantee that this would cease. Second, I wanted to ask the President to release two Australians who had been imprisoned for more than a year in Bangladesh for gold smuggling; it seemed to the Australian Government that it was time they be allowed to return home. The third matter concerned a staff member of the High Commission. The Australians concerned with these problems all knew I was seeing the President and expected me to say something. Not to have done so would have meant a bad start from the perspective of the Australian community. Fortunately, the President listened to what I said and eventually the matters were settled to the satisfaction of the Australians concerned.

Shortly after I presented my credentials, the temperature of political life increased. President Ershad had become increasingly unpopular, largely because of his autocratic methods and because he was believed to be corrupt. Opposition parties consequently became more active in re-iterating their traditional demand that he should stand down, hand over power to a caretaker administration and call fresh elections. As often happens in Bangladesh, political activity became more pronounced during the cooler weather and there were a number of violent demonstrations in October 1990 during which eight people were killed.

I had been planning to take a three week holiday in Korea, Japan and China in November 1990. Some time during October, I cabled the Department of Foreign Affairs and Trade in Canberra stating that the political climate was getting warmer, but that I thought that if anything dramatic happened, it would not occur until 1991 and that I thought I could safely go on leave. The Department concurred and I left on 11 November by air for Tokyo.

By co-incidence President Ershad and his wife were on the same flight travelling to attend the coronation of the new Emperor of Japan. Neither he nor I realised that I would have to cut my holiday short three weeks later because Ershad himself would fall from power. If he had had the slightest premonition of this, he would have remained in Bangladesh to avoid such a catastrophe.

After returning from Japan, and after several fruitless attempts at negotiation with the opposition parties, Ershad resigned from the presidency on 4 December 1990. The army played an important role by refusing to encourage Ershad to remain in power. Another significant factor was the temporary unity of the strong anti-government student movement and of the opposition political parties themselves.

Particularly significant also were the waves of strikes that hit the country. Journalists went on strike; many shops and offices closed; printers went on strike; transportation came to a standstill; doctors and nurses likewise went on strike and, eventually, so did the public service. It seemed that the entire country was ceasing to function.

While most of this was going on, I was on the last leg of my holiday in Korea, and not paying particular attention to developments in Bangladesh, which were not reported widely in other countries. Eventually I received a telephone call from the Department in Canberra to say that I should return to Dhaka. It took some time to arrange the necessary travel and I could not go immediately as I had developed a nasal infection, was under medical treatment and could not safely travel by plane. Eventually, the condition improved and I returned to Dhaka, but only after Ershad had fallen from power.

Another Head of Mission in Dhaka told me that, during this period, he had been asked to accompany Ershad on a short flight to inspect some development project. My colleague was rather reluctant to do this, bearing in mind the degree of hostility to Ershad that had already manifested itself. Thinking of the ill-fated plane trip undertaken by President Zia of Pakistan together with the American Ambassador to Pakistan a few years earlier, in which both had been killed, my colleague wondered whether he would return. He carefully explained to his wife what official and personal steps she should take if he did not return, a somewhat morbid precaution. Fortunately, the expedition proved a safe one.

The fall of Ershad was the second demonstration of "people

power" that I had witnessed, the first being the overthrow of Syngman Rhee in Korea in 1960. It seemed strange that I should have had this experience in my first and last posts. Despite current talk about "Asian values" (often used as a mere screen for dictatorship and corruption), there are some standards that are world-wide and that people insist on being met. Regimes seen and known to be corrupt cannot last forever, no matter how long they do last. People will insist on having some say, eventually, in how they are governed.

After the fall of Ershad, attention focussed on the leaders of the two main opposition parties – Sheikh Hasina and Khaleda Zia. Sheikh Hasina, the President of the Awami League, was the daughter of the assassinated first Prime Minister of Bangladesh, Sheikh Mujib Rahman. Begum Zia, the Chairman (sic) of the Bangladesh National Party, was the widow of the former, assassinated President of Bangladesh and founder of the Bangladesh National Party (the BNP), Ziaur Rahman.

They both had attractive personal qualities, as anyone who had met them knew. Another positive factor was their relative youth in contrast to some of the older leaders, especially in the Awami League. On the other hand, neither had experience in government and Begum Zia's educational background was very limited.

Begum Zia was born on 15 August 1945, the day the war in the Pacific ended. She was married at the age of 13 in 1958 to Ziaur Rahman and had given birth to two children. She had had some secondary education but, throughout her married life, President Zia had kept her very much in the background and she had not participated in politics until she became Chairman of the BNP in 1984. She did not have any executive experience (apart from her party duties) until she became Prime Minister in 1991.

Sheikh Hasina, born on 28 September 1947, had married Dr M. A. Mazed Miah in 1969. She graduated as Bachelor of Arts from Dhaka University and had been President of the Awami

Richard Gate with Begum Khaleda Zia, Prime Minister of Bangladesh, 1992

League since 1981. She and her sister, who were abroad at the time, were the only two members of Sheikh Mujib's family who survived his assassination on 15 August 1975 by discontented army officers. Both Sheikh Hasina and Begum Zia entered politics because of their family background rather than as a result of any talent or ambition for leadership. To some extent, Begum Zia, a calmer and more dignified figure, seemed to have grown into her role more than had Sheikh Hasina whose determination to bring her father's murderers to justice suggested that her main concern was with the past.

Both leaders faced the traditional distaste in Islam for women leaders. But South Asia had grown accustomed in recent years to the idea of strong women prime ministers and there was no male in sight who could challenge either Begum Zia or Sheikh Hasina within their respective parties.

In the High Commission, we kept in touch with all the political leaders during the period that led up to the fall of Ershad and afterwards. Senator Gareth Evans, the Foreign Minister, visited Bangladesh in August 1990 and saw not only President Ershad but also Sheikh Hasina and Begum Zia. I had called on both leaders after I arrived in Dhaka and, several months afterwards, I had invited Begum Zia to my residence one evening for dinner and a talk. The fact that Western ambassadors, such as the British, Canadian and American as well as myself, were willing to talk to both women during difficult times gave them, I think, a sense of confidence that they might otherwise not have had.

Begum Zia was not very communicative when I first met her. When Senator Evans visited in 1990, before she became Prime Minister, she preferred to let her chief supporters do the talking. After becoming Prime Minister, she grew in confidence. When I called on her, I usually found that the best way to get across any point I wanted to make was to ask her questions about it, rather than put it to her directly. I found that she always knew what was my purpose and was usually ready with a quick response. If necessary, I could then go on and ask further questions. On particular subjects the depth of her knowledge was impressive. Undoubtedly well briefed, she had a good command of the advice she had received.

With the fall of Ershad, the political scene was transformed completely. An election took place on 27 February 1991. A new government of the Bangladesh National Party with Begum Zia as Prime Minister took office.

Despite the appearance of manifestos by the political parties, the election campaign did not lead to a discussion of fundamental differences among them, but was conducted almost entirely around the record of the governments of Sheikh Mujib Rahman (Sheikh Hasina's father) and President Ziaur Rahman (Begum Zia's husband). Both women hurled insults at the record of the opposing party when in office and said that electors could expect more of the same if they elected that party. Begum Zia disputed Sheikh Hasina's claim that the Awami League had presided over a "Golden Age" in Bangladesh. She claimed that, in those days, "man and dog ate from the same dustbin" and women had to wear fishnets instead of saris.

The Australian High Commission, together with other missions and private organisations, sent out observer teams on election day to judge, insofar as we could, whether the elections were free and fair. All the political parties welcomed this. Our Third Secretary, Felicity Volk, who led one of the teams, had an experience during this election which seemed to epitomise Bangladesh life and the problems of diplomats in Bangladesh. While she was travelling across one of the major rivers on a ferry, a man on the ferry claimed that the Land Rover (driven by a Bangladeshi) in which she (the Third Secretary) was travelling had run over a women's foot and broken it. The man insisted that the Third Secretary and the alleged victim go with him to the police station where the man repeated his allegations. The injured woman denied that our Land Rover had been in any way responsible and said she had previously sustained the injury elsewhere..

By this time, as always happens in Bangladesh after this kind of incident, an enormous crowd had gathered outside and inside the police station and had become hostile towards the foreigners present. The policeman pointed this out and claimed that, even though the woman had denied that the Australian Land Rover was responsible, the Third Secretary would have to pay compensation if she were to get out of the situation unharmed. In the end she paid money (not much) to the injured woman, both as compensation and as a contribution to medical expenses, and to the man who had made the accusations. Only then was she allowed to leave.

I protested to the Foreign Ministry at a very senior level about this extortion from a diplomatic representative. My interlocutor said that he was sorry, but pointed out that something like this could easily occur in Liverpool, England. I replied that episodes like this should not occur anywhere. My representations must have made some impression as I heard later from other officials in the Ministry that the episode had been discussed at one of their senior meetings. Apart from that, I heard nothing more about it. Nevertheless, I did not want the episode to pass unnoticed.

Shortly before the election of February 1991, we had a visit from Senator Robert Hill, then Leader of the Opposition in the Senate and the Liberal Party spokesman on foreign affairs. In one of his conversations with Bangladeshi politicians, Senator Hill stressed that it would be important that the result of the forthcoming election be accepted by all contenders, winners and losers.

Senator Hill was right. The Leader of the Opposition, Sheikh Hasina, the President of the Awami League, never accepted that her party lost the election. She believed that, because it was her father's party that led Bangladesh to independence, any situation in which another party was in government was a dangerous aberration. Any election which the Awami League lost must, she thought, be the result of government manipulation.

The attitude of the Awami League amounted to an assault on the credibility of Bangladesh's political institutions. After the election of 1991, the Awami League did everything it could to bring down the government and force fresh elections. The former Governor-General of Australia, Sir Ninian Stephen, attempted (after I had left Dhaka), on behalf of the Commonwealth Secretariat, to mediate between the government and the opposition and was finally forced to admit defeat. After staging boycotts and walking out of Parliament on many occasions, the Awami

League eventually secured agreement from Begum Zia to hold a fresh election under a caretaker government in 1996; this election resulted in defeat of the BNP Government and installation of an Awami League Government under Sheikh Hasina.

While I was in Bangladesh there was a serious populist movement to hang Professor Golam Azam, the leader of the fundamentalist Jamaat-e-Islami Party on the grounds that he had opposed Bangladesh independence in 1971 and had also, amongst other things, raped 300 women at that time. A special, non-government committee was formed to promote his execution and the leader of this committee declared that "the blessings of Allah will shower on the country when Golam Azam is hanged." A mock trial was staged in a public park, charges were read and the crowd pronounced Golam Azam guilty and demanded his execution. This travesty of justice occupied the country for some months when minds would have been better spent devising ways to ameliorate the condition of the poverty stricken masses.

After I left Bangladesh, the subsequent Awami League Government brought charges against Golam Azam who was, in 2013, convicted of war crimes and sentenced to ninety years in prison. He died in a prison hospital in 2014.

On another occasion, a leading (male) figure in Dhaka's social life contracted a marriage which was considered unsuitable by some. Processions with placards calling for his immediate hanging took place for several days in the main streets.

More serious than these incidents were the violent manifestations of intolerance. "Violence, more than anything else, has created suspicion in the public mind about the credibility of the BNP Government and the future of the representative political system in Bangladesh," a Bangladeshi scholar, Professor Muhammad A. Hakim, wrote in *Bangladeshi Politics: The Shahadbuddin Interregnum* (1993).

Violence was particularly strong in universities and other

educational establishments. Many of the universities were closed at various times for lengthy periods because of student unrest. "Session-jam", a back log of students who had not been able to follow or complete their courses, had created serious administrative problems.

Campus violence did not arise from administrative or academic grievances within the universities, but from an internecine struggle for power within and among student political factions. The Vice Chancellor of Dhaka University, Professor Mia, stated publicly that peace would not return to the campuses until the political parties decided to call off the fighting. The parties were reluctant to do this; they knew that students had been traditionally in the vanguard of political life in Bangladesh and that it would be politically dangerous for them to defang their respective student wings. In the meantime, the demoralised police, who refused to intervene in the student wars because of the protection given to the students by the parties, had become less active generally, leading to a rise in crime and brigandage throughout the country.

Especially active in the field of student terrorism were the JCD, the BNP's student wing, and Shibir, the student wing of the Jamaat-i-Islami Party.

I was invited to attend a function at one of the Residential Halls at Dhaka University in 1991 at the height of the university violence. After consulting members of the High Commission staff, I decided the chances of being shot were too great and declined. This was a great pity as it was very unusual for Heads of Missions to be invited to attend functions of this kind. We finally circumvented the problem to some extent by inviting a representative group of students to my residence for dinner.

But it was not only the students who created political disturbances resulting in violence. The BNP's first three years of office were marked by many industrial strikes and demonstrations brought about by militant unionism. Many of these incidents were held to protest against the Government's economic rationalisation programs and demonstrated its difficulties in balancing, on the one hand, pressure from aid donors to take tough measures and, on the other, the demands of the workers.

When I left Bangladesh in November 1993, it was impossible to say that the level of violence had decreased.

Economic Developments

Surrounded by violence and constant attacks by the Awami League, the new Government of Begum Zia often found it difficult to press on with necessary reforms, particularly in the economic field, a field of interest to Australia.

Our role as a major aid donor meant that Australia was represented, as it had been in the case of Burma, at the annual meeting of the Bangladesh Aid Consortium held each year at the World Bank office in Paris. At these meetings, the Bangladesh Government would explain what problems it had encountered in economic development during the preceding year. The World Bank and Bangladesh's aid donors, such as Australia, would then outline how they thought these problems might be overcome and indicated their aid levels for the coming year. I attended four of these meetings. I was usually the only member of the Australian delegation. I prepared my own brief, composed and delivered my own speeches and wrote my own report of the meeting to the Australian International Development Assistance Bureau (until recently AUSAID).

Essentially, what all Bangladesh governments had been trying to do for the previous fifteen years was to move the country away from the rigid statist economy introduced by the Awami League after independence in 1971. That Government nationalised many industries and instituted a command, protected economy, similar to that of many Third World countries in those years. Like many of them, Bangladesh has had a great deal of trouble in moving away from that model and introducing change.

President Ershad did do some useful work in this respect, but his manipulation of the banking system for his own purposes meant that huge amounts of money that could have been lent for productive purposes were siphoned off for more questionable ends. In the last year of his rule, he vastly increased public expenditure on such things as subsidies, public service wage increases and army costs, and also let foreign exchange reserves slide dramatically.

At the first Paris meeting I attended in 1990, the donors were very critical of the Government and demanded that it introduce an action plan to reverse the serious deterioration in the economy. The action plan was adopted and a mid-term meeting was held in Dhaka in November 1990 at which we found that the Government had to a great extent implemented necessary reforms and that the situation had much improved. Nevertheless, word of Ershad's mismanagement of the economy had got about and the fact that a major meeting of foreigners was held in Dhaka to assess how far the situation had been rectified was one of the reasons for Ershad's fall the following month.

At each of the next three meetings I attended, the new BNP Finance Minister, Saifur Rahman, gave an account of how far he had been able to take Bangladesh down the road of liberalisation. Every year before the meeting, I and the other diplomats who went to Paris would meet at the Canadian High Commissioner's house with the Finance Minister for a preliminary discussion. We also had regular meetings with Ministry of Finance and other officials during the year to discuss specific problems (such as the elimination of poverty, role of women in development, irrigation projects).

In general, by the time I left Bangladesh, there had been many improvements. One was introduction of a Value Added Tax in 1991 which increased government revenues considerably. Another was the lowering of tariffs which made imported components in industry considerably cheaper than before. The major success, already visible during Ershad's years, was the huge increase in grain production due to better seed and greater use of fertiliser; Bangladesh could then produce sufficient grain to meet market demands. (Millions of people, however, were too poor to participate in the market and therefore buy food.)

There were, however, some areas in which the Government had not succeeded. Investment levels remained low. The Government had not succeeded in increasing to the required extent the sums available for public investment under the Annual Development Program. Nor had it created an atmosphere in which private investment, both domestic and foreign, could flourish. There was still too much uncertainty in Bangladesh in all spheres of life, political, economic and social, to permit potential investors to see far enough ahead.

Nor, as in many other countries, had the Government succeeded in disposing of the old, money-losing state corporations. These could not be operated as viable units, nor could they be sold. Any move to do so was resisted by their employees' unions.

Militant unionism was, however surprising it may seem in a country of massive unemployment, very strong in Bangladesh. Politicians traditionally encouraged formation of unions which they then used for partisan purposes. These unions demanded, and received, wage increases that industry could not afford and also imposed other uneconomic conditions.

Although the central economic task of Bangladeshi governments is alleviation of poverty, the incidence of extreme poverty had risen by 1993 when I left the country. The proportion of those unable to afford a daily intake of 1805 calories had risen from 22 per cent of the population in 1985-6 to 27 per cent in 1988-9. In 1990, per capita income was estimated to be only US $220. The literacy rate for all ages by 1993 was only 24.8 per cent. To enable the average poor Bangaldeshi to cross the poverty line, real per capita income had to grow by six or seven per cent for ten years.

The absolute number of poor in Bangladesh had grown every year since independence in 1971. In this respect, the Finance Minister had noted grimly in his 1993 Budget speech that, although he had had many dialogues with various lobbies and interest groups during the preparation of his budget, "in the course of such dialogues I did not have the good fortune to encounter a single lobby which really wants to protect the interests of the teeming millions of the poor common consumers of Bangladesh".

Some improvements had been made. World Bank figures showed that GNP per capita had risen to US $220 in 1992 from US $160 in 1986; 40 per cent of the rural population had access to drinking water in 1980 as compared to 80 per cent in 1992; the per capita intake of protein had risen from 42 grams a day in 1983 to 64 in 1988-89; and 5,304 people were served by one physician in 1992 as opposed to 5,900 in 1983-85. The Government had made serious efforts in its budgets to increase the money available in the health and education sectors. But alleviation of poverty had a long way to go in Bangladesh.

The Gulf War (1990-91)

It was a fascinating experience to live through the 1990-91 Gulf War in Dhaka and realising the implications it had for Bangladesh. There were also some anxious moments.

Bangladesh's response to the Iraqi invasion of Kuwait in August 1990 was prompt. The Government sent a "token" military contingent to Saudi Arabia to join the international force protecting that country. The decision was taken, the Government said, in support of the principle that larger states should not attack smaller states. But it was not an easy decision. Iraq had been for many years one of Bangladesh's closest friends in the Middle

East and any suggestion that Bangladesh was hostile to Iraq could have had serious internal repercussions.

President Ershad also had the difficult task of repatriating 63,233 Bangladeshi workers from the Middle East after the invasion of Kuwait. This was handled very well.

By the time the Gulf War began on 15 January 1991, Ershad had fallen from power. The interim Government was busy organising elections to be held on 27 February. The war turned out to be a distraction, not a major factor in the election.

Nevertheless, popular sentiment was affected. The despatch of the contingent had never been widely supported. Opposition parties and leftist groups attacked the decision as a violation of non-alignment and Bangladesh's neutral foreign policy. Although Ershad had supported the Western coalition, a latent anti-Western feeling among the people not normally noticeable in Bangladesh manifested itself after the war broke out. Saddam Hussein's portrait appeared in many unexpected places, such as on rickshaws. Ordinary Bangladeshi saw the allied effort against Iraq as a Western attack on Islam (forgetting for the moment that Kuwait, Iraq's victim, was also Muslim). Bangladeshi politicians who were electioneering found their meetings deserted when people went home to hear the latest news from the Gulf on their transistors. When I went walking in the afternoons, little children would hiss, "Bush, Bush", at me. Westerners stayed away from places they otherwise might have frequented such as video rental stores. We had to cancel the Australia Day reception on 26 January. The High Commission office was stoned by a mob in the pay of the Iraqi Embassy. The recreation centre in the American Embassy was badly damaged. For a while we had guards on both my residence and the office.

One evening during this crisis I asked six other Heads of Mission to my house to discuss the situation. They all came at different times and sent their cars home immediately. We felt that if our presence together had become known, it could have been a target for hostile demonstrations.

We had to consider seriously the possibility of the evacuation of Australians. In accordance with normal practice in such circumstances, we instituted a nation-wide warden system, giving one Australian in each major area responsibility for keeping in touch with all Australians, so we would know where they were and would be able to issue any warnings if necessary. We advised any Australians who might be planning to leave the country to do so without delay. I secured permission from our Foreign Minister to send any non-essential staff and families out of Bangladesh if necessary. Fortunately, the need for this did not arise.

One of the Ershad Government's reasons for supporting the United Nations' action in Kuwait was its defence of the principle that a small country (Kuwait) should not be invaded by a large country (Iraq) – a very important principle for Bangladesh to defend because of Bangladesh's fear of India. But this reasoning was not universally accepted, even by intelligent and educated Bangladeshis. One night at a dinner party at my residence, a retired, very senior official of the Bangladeshi foreign service, who was very much opposed to the Western role in the Gulf crisis and Bangladesh's part in it, argued that the large/small country analogy was false. Kuwait, he argued, was not a small country because its enormous wealth gave it potential clout and strength far beyond similar countries of comparable size. Although this view seemed rather eccentric to me, I suspect many Bangladeshis supported it.

In a major stroke of good fortune, the war ended on the day of the election – 27 February 1991. The new Government was thus spared the task of formulating a policy towards it and the war itself was forgotten in the euphoric post-election period. The anti-Western manifestations evaporated overnight.

Human Rights in Bangladesh

World-wide observance of human rights is a matter to which Australian governments attach conspicuous importance. I was therefore often asked to report on human rights matters in Bangladesh and to make representations to the Bangladesh Government on human rights questions.

Human rights have long been a difficult issue in Bangladesh. Poverty, over-population, illiteracy and the violent nature of Bangladeshi politics have never been conducive to establishment of a safe breeding ground for the observance of human rights.

Constitutional Rights

Bangladesh governments have traditionally recognised the existence of human rights and have supported them, at least in theory. The Constitution provides for freedom of speech, subject only to "reasonable restrictions". The governments of President Zia, President Ershad and Begum Zia generally allowed the press to operate freely.

Freedom of religion is enshrined in the Constitution. As an estimated 87 per cent of the population is Islamic, members of other religions often feel insecure as a result of communal tensions and the dislike among Moslems of conversion from Islam. Non-Moslems often resent the intrusive nature of Islam and believe that their status has been adversely affected by the amendment to the Constitution in 1988 establishing Islam as the State religion. Minorities are disadvantaged in access to government jobs and political office.

One of the problems I had was with Australian Baptists working in Bangladesh. The Baptist religion had been introduced very early into Bangladesh and was well-established, even though the number of Baptists was not very great in Bangladeshi terms. There had been a long association with Australian Baptists, some of whom were always stationed in Bangladesh. Because proselytising is not allowed, these people were not missionaries in the strict sense, but rather church administrators. There was, nevertheless, some suspicion of them. It was often difficult for the Australian Baptists to get visas for Bangladesh and, once there, they could not leave without an exit permit which was almost as difficult to get. One Australian was banned from re-entering the country while I was there. I often had to ring the Home Minister himself to get visas or exit permits granted. I never discovered what was the real problem that the Government had about Baptists.

The two main human rights questions that I had to deal with in Bangladesh concerned refugee, racial and tribal problems. One was the influx of refugees from Burma in 1991 and the other was the difficult problem in the Chittagong Hill Tracts.

Influx of Burmese Refugees 1991-93

The problems caused by the influx of Burmese refugees, known as the Rohingyas, into Bangladesh, which has caused much comment in recent years, is by no means new. Approximately 250,000 Moslem refugees came into Bangladesh from Burma beginning in mid-1991. The refugees claimed they had been forced out of Burma by the Burmese army in an "ethnic cleansing" campaign and that, before being expelled, they had been forced to work without remuneration for the army in various development projects. The refugees were obviously from the very poorest sections of Burmese society.

The Burmese Government claimed that the refugees were originally illegal migrants from Bangladesh who had fled Burma for Bangladesh when the Burmese authorities had tried to check their papers. The Burmese Government at first showed very little interest in accepting them back.

The Bangladesh Government, although at first giving refuge to these fellow-Moslems, soon grew tired of them, claiming that they were occupying valuable land, cutting down trees, destroying the ecology of the area (a small strip of land just south of Chittagong in the extreme south-east corner of Bangladesh), driving up the price of rice and introducing all kinds of social problems. Eventually, the Bangladesh Government's main object-ive was to get rid of the refugees as soon as possible.

It at first tried to solve the problem bilaterally with Burma, but without success. It then "internationalised" the question and called on the United Nations High Commissioner for Refugees (UNHCR) for help in taking care of the refugees and in repatriating them.

Rohingya refugees arriving in Bangladesh, 1992

In the 1990s, refugee issues had come to achieve a degree of importance they had not had in earlier years and the international community was unwilling to see the refugees return to Burma unless they, the refugees, did so voluntarily. The refugees themselves would not return until they knew that conditions of safety and security existed in Burma and that they would not again be mistreated as they had been before. They could not be sure of this unless the Burmese allowed a United Nations presence on the Burmese side to monitor the situation there. This the Burmese refused to do. The refugees in turn refused to return.

Eventually, after the Burmese Government had agreed to accept some refugees, the Bangladesh Government started to force the refugees out of Bangladesh and into Burma, merely to dispose of a pressing social problem. This led to disturbances in the refugee camps in which some people were killed, and to expressions of international concern. Many discussions, in which I participated, took place between diplomatic missions in Dhaka and the Bangladesh Government. The diplomats urged the Government that the refugees should not return to Burma unless a representative of the UNHCR certified that they were willing to return. The High Commissioner for Refugees herself, Mrs Ogata, echoed these calls and indicated that she could not continue to be associated with the repatriation unless satisfactory arrangements were made.

Eventually, various arrangements were made between the Bangladesh Government and the UNHCR which permitted the UNHCR to interview the refugees in certain circumstances, but, because the Burmese still refused to allow a UNHCR presence on their side of the border to monitor the situation, very few refugees returned there. This led the exasperated Bangladeshis to resort once more to forced repatriation in the face of the objections of the UNHCR, the United Nations General Assembly and diplomatic missions in Dhaka, including our own.

I, and the rest of the staff, devoted much time to this issue. We made many trips to the area where the refugees were to assess the situation. We participated in many meetings with the office of the United Nations High Commissioner for Refugees (UNHCR) and other international organisations. I had many discussions at senior level with the Foreign Ministry and other ministries designed to ascertain what was happening and to explain the Australian Government's position. Our main concern was to support the UNHCR in its insistence that proper procedures should be followed in handling repatriation of the refugees. The problem had certainly not been solved by the time I left Bangladesh. As recent developments have shown, it still has not been solved.

The episode was also significant in that, for the first time, Bangladesh was subject to a degree of international criticism on a social problem. Previously, Bangladesh had become accustomed to attracting international sympathy and support in situations such as the 1991 cyclone. This time, however, Bangladesh realised that some of its own actions can attract criticism.

Chittagong Hill Tracts

Bangladesh is a largely homogeneous nation. About 99 per cent of the population is Bengali and speak that language; about 87 per cent of the population is Moslem. The Chittagong Hill Tracts (CHT) are the major exception to this homogeneity. This area, in south-eastern Bangladesh and bordered by the Indian states of Tripura and Mizoram, is about 5,093 square miles and comprises about one-tenth of the land area of Bangladesh. Unlike the rest of Bangladesh, which is largely flat, the CHT consist to a large extent of hills and forests. The inhabitants are of Sino-Tibetan origin and resemble more the Burmese than the Bengalis. There are thirteen tribes in the CHT, each speaking its own dialect or language. Few of them are Moslems; most are Buddhists, Christians, or animists. Their culture is very different from that of the Bengali Moslems.

The British had always respected the distinct nature of the people in the CHT and had not interfered with their tribal life. When the Indian sub-continent was partitioned in 1947, the inhabitants of the CHT wanted to join India, but were prevented from doing so and became part of (East) Pakistan. Thereafter there has been constant trouble in the CHT.

The main cause of discontent was migration to that area by Bengalis from elsewhere in Bangladesh. The sparsely populated Hill Tracts had always attracted Bengalis from the more closely settled parts of Bangladesh. In 1947 the tribals constituted 98 per cent of the population of the CHT, the Bengalis less than two per cent. By 1981, the tribals accounted for only 58 per cent. Bengali population in the CHT rose to nine per cent in 1951, 12 per cent in 1961, and 40 per cent in 1981. This migration was actively promoted by the Government of President Ziaur Rahman in the late 1970s and early 1980s. The tribals claimed that their own land was confiscated and given to the Bengali settlers.

In 1993 there were approximately one million people living in the CHT; that is, less than one per cent of the population occupying ten per cent of the land of the entire nation. These statistics have made it difficult to argue with the Bangladesh Government's proposition that all Bangladeshis should be free to settle in any part of their own country, particularly if the area in question is less closely settled than the rest of the country. Article 36 of the Constitution gives every citizen the right "to move freely, reside and settle" in any part of Bangladesh. The Government made it clear that it was unwilling to alter the Constitution to restrict the movement of Bengalis into the CHT.

The tribal leaders in the mid-1970s went underground and organised the Shanti Bahini, an insurgent group which engaged in armed struggle. There were frequent confrontations between it and the security forces in the ensuing years. The Shanti Bahini often attacked Bengali settlers and those tribals who, it believed, sympathised with them. Attacks by the Shanti Bahini on Bengali settlements often led to reprisal raids against innocent tribal villagers. To some extent, the traditional life-style of the tribals was seriously endangered by this fighting.

The Shanti Bahini demanded autonomy for the CHT. The

Government rejected this demand, arguing that the peculiar circumstances of Bangladesh demanded that it be a unitary state, not one burdened with autonomous regions which could not easily survive.

Successive governments of Bangladesh tried to solve the problem by military means and established a considerable military presence in the area. The military became the administrators of the CHT, much to the resentment of the tribals.

As a result of the fighting, many tribals took refuge in the Indian state of Tripura. By 1988, India claimed there were over 45,000 refugees in Tripura; by 1990 this number had risen to 60,000.

The question of India's relationship with the refugees in Tripura had always been a difficult one. The official Indian position was that the CHT dispute remained an internal one for Bangladesh to solve, but that the Indian Government abided by the rules set down by the United Nations in dealing with refugees. India would not compel the refugees to return; if they returned, it had to be of their own volition. Meanwhile, India pointed out, it was meeting the cost of feeding the refugees.

The Bangladesh Government accused India of siding with and abetting the Shanti Bahini, particularly by providing shelter for them in India and also by arming them. The Government claimed that the Shanti Bahini forced the refugees to remain in the camps and used the refugee issue to maintain pressure on Bangladesh.

This situation led over the years to many accusations by human rights groups in the West that human rights violations were being perpetrated by the army in the CHT. Most of the changes in Bangladesh official policy in the late 1980s and afterwards were in response, not to internal pressures, but to the demands of Western donor nations, motivated to a great extent by human rights groups. Australian parliamentarians showed a great interest in the CHT and the High Commission was required to keep the Department well-informed about conditions there.

In February 1990, shortly after arriving in Bangladesh, I visited the CHT. Throughout the visit, I was accompanied by a police escort of eight armed men, belying the repeated official line that security had been all but restored to the CHT. In a military briefing in Chittagong, I was told that India was intent on destabilising Bangladesh and that this was to be achieved in part by inciting the tribals to seek autonomy and by providing arms to the Shanti Bahini. According to the briefing, the Shanti Bahini then numbered 7,000, of whom 5,000 were trained and 1,500 armed.

The impression I received during the visit was that, as long as the insurgents continued to refuse adamantly to negotiate with the Government on any package which excluded their ill-defined concept of autonomy, a compromise solution would never be reached.

Members of the High Commission made many visits to the CHT and consideration of the CHT problem absorbed a great deal of our time. None of us thought that there seemed to be any real progress in solving the major problem: the refugees would not return from Tripura unless they thought that they would be returning to stable and prosperous conditions which could not be assured so long as the army still governed the CHT and the problems posed by the presence of the Bengali settlers had not been solved. Even if the refugees had been willing to return, the Shanti Bahini probably would not have let them do so unless the Shanti Bahini's preposterous demands for autonomy for the CHT had been met.

A Committee of Parliamentarians was established in 1992 to negotiate directly with the Shanti Bahini (not the refugees) and make recommendations to the Government for a solution of the political problems in the CHT. In its negotiations with the Shanti Bahini, the Committee assured them that their lands and homes would be returned to them if a negotiated settlement took place. In addition, no more Bengalis would be allowed to settle in the

CHT. But the Committee could not accede to CHT demands for autonomy and that the Bengali settlers be expelled.

The Shanti Bahini replied that there could not be any settlement of problems in the CHT until the authorities accepted the Shanti Bahini's demand for a fully autonomous region after the withdrawal of security forces and for all Bengali settlers to be expelled.

Despite this impasse, the Bangladesh Government tried to speed things up. A visit to the camps in Tripura in May 1993 by the Indian Minister of State for External Affairs and a Bangladeshi Minister led to a joint statement that repatriation would begin within thirty days. There was no evidence that it did. As might have been expected, on the date on which repatriation was due to begin arrived, 8 June 1993, only one refugee crossed the border. From reports received from India, it appeared that the refugees told the Indian authorities that they would not return until their demands were met. Whatever the truth, it was at least evident that the Indian authorities were not resorting to forced repatriation.

Stephen Gee, Second Secretary from the High Commission, visited the CHT in October 1993. He found that little progress had been made in the peace talks. Neither side had conceded anything. The tribals were still demanding that the Bengali settlers be expelled, that the army be removed, and that an autonomous region in the CHT be created. The Government rejected these demands, but was itself dragging out the negotiations. A solution seemed far off.

I left Bangladesh in November 1993. It is very easy to overstate the tribals' case and to over-criticise the Bangladesh Government on the CHT issue. In my advice to the Australian Government I took care to balance two conflicting factors. On the one hand, there was no use denying that deplorable incidents of terrorism had occurred or that many of the tribals in the CHT had been driven off their land. On the other hand, I did not urge that Australia support the tribals' demand for autonomy and that all the Bengalis who had settled in the CHT be expelled. Neither of these proposals was realistic.

I found officials in the Foreign Ministry willing to receive my representations about the CHT. They knew that Bangladesh had a problem in presenting this problem to the world and what they said to me was reasonable enough. On occasion, I found them too willing to believe that, just because the Bangladesh and Indian governments wanted the refugees to return to Bangladesh, they would do so. Only under pressure would they admit that "the refugees will return when they are ready to do so."

Long after I left Bangladesh, a peace accord was signed by the new Awami League Government and the political wing of the Shanti Bahini in 1997. The subsequent BNP Government of 2001 promised to implement the accord. The 2018 Amnesty International Report on Bangladesh contains references to attacks on indigenous people in the CHT and of solders using excessive force against students.

Other Human Rights Problems

Amnesty International and other groups have frequently been critical of the human rights situation in Bangladesh. In its 1993 report on Bangladesh, Amnesty International claimed that prisoners of conscience had been arrested and detained; that torture continued to be widespread, particularly of persons in police custody; that extra-judicial executions by security forces continued to take place, especially in the Chittagong Hill Tracts; that the death penalty continued to be imposed; and that political and criminal violence continued at a high level.

The reports issued each year by the United States State Department on human rights in Bangladesh also contained some of these charges.

I had many discussions with senior Bangladeshi officials about these reports as I was required to keep Canberra informed about the human rights situation in Bangladesh. Some of the officials I spoke to were amazingly frank in off-the-record comments. They all admitted that reports such as Amnesty International's were useful in bringing certain matters to light and in providing a basis for discussion. They certainly did not claim that Amnesty's or other reports were fabricated, deliberately unfair to Bangladesh, or that the human rights situation in Bangladesh was perfect.

They did, nevertheless, claim that things were not always as Amnesty or other outsiders saw them.

Although the Constitution forbade torture, some officials admitted that it sometimes took place. They claimed, however, that sometimes the police bribed the victims to remain silent. The Police Association might also destroy evidence of torture which meant that the case could not be heard.

Extra-judicial killings often took place, but it was not always the police who were responsible. Some deaths were caused by students themselves during student demonstrations. If a student responsible for a death belonged to one of the major political parties, it was difficult for the police to proceed against him.

The death penalty was still on the books in Bangladesh and representations were often made to the Government by representatives of other governments and organisations like Amnesty International that it be abolished. On several occasions I had to make representations to the Foreign Ministry and ask that a death sentence not be implemented.

The Government's reply to these representations was that the death penalty would remain in the statute books in Bangladesh as long as the public accepted it. There can be little doubt that the public did, on the whole, accept the death penalty. Political figures in Bangladesh frequently called for the execution of their opponents and others whom they thought deserved it. Bangladeshis showed great interest when murderers were hanged, often demanding to see the bodies, and it was clear that there was much support for such executions. It was unrealistic to expect that, in the then circumstances, the death penalty would be abolished.

In dealing with human rights questions, Bangladesh faced unusual problems. Poverty breeds crime and the Government was under constant pressure to eliminate blackmail, extortion, theft, murder, rape and other violent crimes. Incompetent police investigatory methods led prosecutors to take short cuts to secure convictions. The Government had taken steps to fight crime more expeditiously, but unfortunately these steps often resulted, or seemed to result, in violations of human rights. The authorities were certainly aware of the problem and there seemed to be little deliberate violation of human rights, at least at higher levels of government, for party political reasons under the BNP regime which governed Bangladesh for most of my time there.

*****

I was able to report to Canberra when I left Bangladesh late in 1993 that some political progress had been made since the overthrow of the Ershad Government. Political institutions, which had been severely damaged during the Ershad years, had to some extent been reconstructed.

Parliament was more politically representative in 1993 because all major parties were in it, as they had not been in Ershad's time. It had become much more the focus of political life than under Ershad. Important legislation had been passed and there were debates in Parliament. Nevertheless, Parliament had still a long way to go. Much of the debate that did take place concerned what seem to be old or peripheral issues, such as the indemnity granted to the murderers of Sheikh Mujib Rahman and the possible trial of Golam Azam. The real problems of Bangladesh, such as the economy and population questions, received much less immediate attention.

Many of the members of Parliament did not comprehend the proper functions of an MP. They interfered in micro-matters of public administration, such as the letting of government tenders. The establishment of a parliamentary committee to investigate charges of corruption against the Minister for Agriculture went nowhere for nearly a year because the committee was unable to decide its own terms of reference. Members sometimes gave the impression that they were unable to deal adequately with matters that they themselves considered of fundamental importance.

The Parliament lacked a proper secretariat and members did not have access to information that would enable them to play their role more effectively. Nor did members have sufficient personal staff. More important than any of these considerations was the fact that the major political parties still seemed to believe that political battles could be waged in the streets and not in Parliament. Both major parties (and the Jamaat) maintained armed factions (especially student groups) to fight these battles.

Begum Zia had emerged as a strong leader within her own party and with wide appeal. Her charisma gave her an advantage over her ministers, none of whom had much popular appeal, and they knew it. But Begum Zia, despite her best intentions, had been unable to move the country sufficiently ahead or put into dramatic effect all the sensible and pragmatic policies which her government had adopted.

The public service had been subject to almost constant personnel changes since the new government assumed office. Whether this was because of personal favouritism or because the Government was having difficulty finding the right people for the right jobs was hard to say, but the effect had been most disruptive. Another problem was the early retiring age of 57: no sooner did a senior man (and there were no women) secure a responsible position than he had to retire. Across the horizon was the eventual disappearance of those officers who were trained in the Pakistani civil service with its superior tradition (at least in those formative years). Bangladesh needed a smaller, better paid and better trained public service, but any Bangladeshi government would find it hard to implement large scale shedding of public service jobs.

The army, certainly under the then Chief of Staff, General Nooruddin, had accepted the principle that no useful purpose would be served by seizing power. The army knew that it did not have answers to Bangladesh's many problems and the fate of former President Ershad, who himself seized power when head of the army, was always there to discourage any usurper. But a bid for power by an ambitious or irrational colonel or general could never be completely ruled out.

Educational institutions unfortunately were still subject to a large degree of political violence resulting in the deaths of and injuries to many students and closure for long periods of the universities, colleges and schools. This was particularly regrettable as education was one of the keys to Bangladesh's future.

Since the fall of Ershad, Bangladesh had jumped over many hurdles that were expected to be insurmountable. The conduct of the election in 1991, the constitutional amendments and the cyclone that year were events which, at the time, seemed to present almost insoluble problems. That they were surmounted successfully proves that solutions to difficult problems could be found in Bangladesh.

In to-day's world, when international interest in an Asian country seems to depend on how much money can be made there, Bangladesh does not rank high on anyone's list. The Bangladeshis have been partly responsible for this by their inability to maintain political stability and the lack of wisdom in their economic policies, at least in the early years of the country's existence. But the 160 million people in Bangladesh, many of them extremely poor, will not go away and they demand the attention not only of their own government (which they do not always get), but of responsible governments everywhere.

11

Afterlife

I left Dhaka in late 1993 and returned to the Department from which I retired several weeks later. Nevertheless, the Department did ask me to undertake some consultancies for the next two years which made the cessation from work less sudden.

When I am asked what was my favourite post, I always reply "Rome". This seems the logical choice because of the cultural richness of Italy and the interesting political and economic developments I encountered there, as well as the attractions of the Italian people.

Nevertheless, I enjoyed all my postings and, in Rome, I often used to say that I had experienced more rewarding evenings of conversation in Nauru than I did in Rome. This may have been because in small posts a diplomat is closer to the political events that are taking place than in a larger metropolitan city.

The post I probably enjoyed least was Jordan. I felt isolated by the thinness of our relations with that country and because of the dismissive attitude of the government towards foreign representatives. The archaeological and historical sites in Jordan and the neighbouring countries did, however, provide some compensations and I have always found the Middle East an attractive area.

I never had the serious trouble with colleagues in the posts in which I served or with accommodation, servants or the transport of my effects, problems which bedevilled many of my colleagues. A good deal of grizzling went on because conditions were not seen to be as good as they had been in previous years, but I do not recall any one time when people said: "Conditions are really good right now". The Golden Era always seemed to be some time in the past or in a future which never seemed to come.

I consider myself lucky in the nine postings – in North Asia, South Asia, South-East Asia, the Middle East, Europe, Africa and the Pacific. The only continent I missed out on was the Americas and, in fact, I had spent my teenage years in New York. I understand that, for diverse reasons, postings are not as easy to secure as they were in my day and I remain grateful to have had the opportunities I did have.

Acknowledgements

In the preparation of this book I am grateful to the following:

The Honourable Thomas M. Thawley for the Foreword,
John Nethercote for invaluable editorial assistance,
Michael Gilchrist for typesetting and layout,
Department of Foreign Affairs and Trade for assistance with photographs.

Richard Gate
Canberra
April 2019

www.ingramcontent.com/pod-product-compliance
Lightning Source LLC
Chambersburg PA
CBHW060954230426
43665CB00015B/2191